UNEQUAL LESSONS

Unequal Lessons

*School Diversity and
Educational Inequality
in New York City*

Alexandra Freidus

NEW YORK UNIVERSITY PRESS
New York

NEW YORK UNIVERSITY PRESS
New York
www.nyupress.org

© 2025 by New York University
All rights reserved

    Please contact the Library of Congress for Cataloging-in-Publication data.

ISBN: 9781479827800 (hardback)
ISBN: 9781479827817 (paperback)
ISBN: 9781479827831 (library ebook)
ISBN: 9781479827824 (consumer ebook)

This book is printed on acid-free paper, and its binding materials are chosen for strength and durability. We strive to use environmentally responsible suppliers and materials to the greatest extent possible in publishing our books.

Manufactured in the United States of America

10 9 8 7 6 5 4 3 2 1

Also available as an ebook

To Ari and Lew, who remind me,

"You can't just say something is a problem.

You have to do something about it!"

CONTENTS

Introduction: "There Is No Magic" in Diversity ... 1

1. "We Weren't Special to Him": Whiteness and Potential Diversity in New York City Schools ... 15

2. Problem Children and Children with Problems: Learning from Diversity at P.S. 411 ... 45

3. What Is Taught and What Is Learned: Lessons from an Antiracist, Integrating Middle School ... 75

4. "A True History of America": Civic Learning through Youth Organizing for School Integration ... 107

Conclusion ... 141

Acknowledgments ... 153

Appendix: Methodological Reflections ... 157

Notes ... 169

Bibliography ... 177

Index ... 191

About the Author ... 199

Introduction

"There Is No Magic" in Diversity

Theoretically, the Negro needs neither segregated schools nor mixed schools. What he needs is Education. What he must remember is that there is no magic, either in mixed schools or in segregated schools. A mixed school with poor and unsympathetic teachers, with hostile public opinion, and no teaching of truth concerning black folk, is bad. A segregated school with ignorant placeholders, inadequate equipment, poor salaries, and wretched housing, is equally bad. Other things being equal, the mixed school is the broader, more natural basis for the education of all youth. It gives wider contacts; it inspires greater self-confidence; and suppresses the inferiority complex. But other things are seldom equal.
—W. E. B. Du Bois, "Does the Negro Need Separate Schools?" (1935)

In 2007, New York City schools chancellor Joel Klein called a plan to desegregate a Brooklyn middle school "unnecessary" and "anachronistic."[1] In 2018, schools chancellor Richard Carranza argued that "diversity is a positive" when he retweeted a viral video titled "Wealthy White Manhattan Parents Angrily Rant against Plan to Bring More Black Kids to Their Schools."[2] In 2022, schools chancellor David Banks described efforts to integrate schools as "playing around on the margins."[3] None of these leaders of the nation's largest public school system disputed the fact that New York City schools are extremely segregated. However, they took very different positions on the question of whether that segregation is a significant problem. Almost ninety years after W. E. B. Du Bois explained that there is "no magic" in either segregated or mixed schools, the debate over school diversity persists. How are we still having this argument? What are we even arguing about?

I came to this book with questions that had been nagging at me for over a decade, since I first started teaching social studies at Berkeley High School. Berkeley High is famous (or notorious, depending on your point of view) for its extreme diversity *and* extreme inequality. During my time there, I learned a great deal from faculty and staff, many of whom worked far outside of school hours to support their students. I engaged with gifted and dedicated colleagues who built authentic learning communities that crossed racial and socioeconomic boundaries; I pestered them with endless questions about how I could do the same in my own classroom. But it often felt close to impossible to counter the inequality that pervaded our school and society. I spent many evenings in angry tears, deeply frustrated by our collective failure to serve Black students really well. I grieved as I watched both adults and kids resist persistent injustice on a daily basis, and I knew that their experience was consistent with national trends.

Like many educators, I hoped our school's racial and socioeconomic diversity might offer an opportunity to work for educational justice. After several years, however, I found myself wondering when, how, and whether such a thing was possible. I ended up teaching for one more year at a selective private high school in the Bay Area because I wondered whether racial patterns might differ in a smaller organization with abundant resources. Spoiler alert: they did not.

After a decade of working in Bay Area schools, I moved to New York City and took a position leading professional development in schools that served almost exclusively low-income Black and Latine students. I spent much of my time observing these segregated classrooms and thinking about how I would like to see them change. After three years, I left my job to begin doctoral studies in education. By then, my own son was one year old. On playdates and in public parks, I listened as White parents very much like myself discussed whether they would send their children to public schools in our gentrifying neighborhood. I paid careful attention to how families described local schools and the students who attended them; I wondered about the implications for students, schools, and educational equity.

During my first year of graduate school, I encountered Du Bois's essay "Does the Negro Need Separate Schools?" When I read *The Souls of Black Folk* as an undergraduate, I had been struck by how deftly Du Bois illuminated "the problem of the color-line" in the United States; his work helped me understand the ways that racialized resource allocation and identity development continue to shape our society. I was therefore not surprised to learn that Du Bois's critique of debates over school segregation still rang true, eighty years after publication. I eagerly read as Du Bois questioned the value of integration—a goal I had long taken for granted. I underlined the criteria that he outlined for "the proper education of any people": "sympathetic touch between teacher and pupil; knowledge on the part of the teacher, not simply of the individual taught, but of his surroundings and background, and the history of his class and group; such contact between pupils, and between teacher and pupil, on the basis of perfect social equality, as will increase this sympathy and knowledge; facilities for education in equipment and housing, and the promotion of such extra-curricular activities as will tend to induct the child into life."[4] This sentence made me think long and hard. Which, if any, of the many schools that I had worked in met these standards? Like Du Bois, I believed that racially diverse schools *could* offer young people a "broader, more natural basis" for learning. Yet I knew that many teachers, including myself, found it very challenging to create a classroom community in which "other things" were equal, and I had witnessed Black students suffering in our extremely diverse school.

Reflecting on my professional and personal experiences, I grew skeptical of parents and colleagues who viewed diversity or school integration as a straightforward response to racial inequality. As a teacher, I recognized the diverse backgrounds and worldviews that kids brought into my classroom and knew that I could take nothing for granted, which was simultaneously a pedagogical asset and an instructional challenge. Once I became a parent, I came to see racial diversity as an experience from which my children might absorb multiple lessons, some of which I wanted them to learn and some of which I did not. Now that I have spent over a decade studying school segregation, integration, and diversity, I have learned to ask new questions: What—and whom—is diversity for? How can educational policy and practice address the costs as well as the benefits of integration? Can diversity and integration move us closer to educational justice?

The Hidden Curriculum of Diversity

Most contemporary approaches to school diversity are rooted in historical efforts to desegregate public education. Black advocates spent decades fighting for their communities' rights; they brought *Brown v. Board of Education* to the Supreme Court after deciding that the only way their children would ever gain access to the educational resources they deserved was if they went to school with White students.[5] However, the Supreme Court decision in *Brown* focused not only on access to "tangible" educational resources, such as safe buildings and legible textbooks, but also on "intangible" resources, such as the White students presumed to serve as Black students' role models. Denying Black students access to this intangible resource, the Court wrote, "generates a feeling of inferiority as to their status in the community that may affect their hearts and minds in a way unlikely ever to be undone."[6] The *Brown* decision thus rests on the perceived deficits of Black children.

This idea that Black kids need to sit next to White kids in order to succeed is implicit in many recent arguments for school diversity. In the sociologist John Diamond's words, contemporary diversity advocates often fail to recognize that "integration was a means to an end—a compromise in a white supremacist system in which white racial actors monopolized educational and other vital resources for their own children."[7]

This compromise has resulted in lasting tensions. On the one hand, we know that desegregation is one of the most effective ways to redistribute material resources among schools, ensuring more equitable access for children who need them.[8] On the other hand, we also know that attempts to diversify schools typically center the preferences, experiences, and priorities of White students and their families.[9] As a result, children of color—and in particular Black children—have long borne the burden of "integrating" White spaces, a process that has inflicted significant racial harm.[10] If, like Du Bois, we believe that a proper education requires *both* adequate "facilities for education" *and* "perfect social equality," this tension is difficult to resolve.

The assumption that increasing student diversity has only positive effects ignores the inequality that permeates many racially and socioeconomically diverse schools. Multiracial schools have the potential to increase children's cultural flexibility, or their capacity to cross social boundaries. They also can dramatically improve students' academic outcomes.[11] However, they often fail to do so. Decades of research demonstrate that White and Asian American students in racially and socioeconomically diverse schools generally take more advanced classes and maintain higher grade point averages (GPAs) than their Black and Latine classmates do. In contrast, Black and Latine students are more likely to be suspended, expelled, and targeted by informal school disciplinary processes.[12] Integration has costs, as well as benefits.

These costs and benefits matter a great deal, of course, to the children involved, to their families, and to their communities. They also affect other students who attend these schools. Children learn from observing and participating in our unequal systems. In diverse schools, as in all schools, students and staff engage in interactions that send powerful messages about where people belong in social hierarchies. Children pay attention to trends in academic achievement, discipline, and peer relationships, and—like adults—they draw conclusions about the causes of these patterns.[13] Diverse or integrated schools thus reflect, reproduce, reinforce, and (in rare moments) resist the existing racial order.

School diversity and integration are, above all, what the sociologists Michael Omi and Howard Winant have called "racial projects." Omi and Winant define a racial project as "simultaneously an interpretation, representation, or explanation of racial identities and meanings, and an effort to organize and distribute resources along particular racial lines."[14] They argue that race is neither a fixed reality nor a meaningless illusion; it is a system of oppression that "plays a fundamental role in structuring and representing the social world."[15] Schools are a central site for this work.

Diversity and integration projects may attempt to intervene in the unequal status quo, but they also structure our racial identities and meanings. They do so in ways that are both highly local (for a person to identify as Asian American or Black means different things at different points in time and different parts of the country) and rooted in broader policies and policy discourses (the meanings of these identities shift in response to, for example, Supreme Court decisions about affirmative action policies). As Diamond reminds us, the original plaintiffs and advocates in the *Brown* case viewed integration as one strategy they could use to approach the broader goal of racial equality. When people argue *for* diverse or integrated schools, their advocacy is often based on the goal of redistributing, in the Supreme Court's words, tangible resources. At the same time, contemporary integration advocates—like the *Brown* decision itself—often rely on deficit-based assumptions about intangible resources. For example, when advocates argue that diversity will benefit low-income students of color, they often implicitly define those students as lacking intellectual, community, or cultural resources.

Some researchers, educators, and advocates seem to see integration as somehow magical: they argue that diverse schools offer unique opportunities for social learning and educational equality.[16] Others argue that segregation is not the underlying cause of the problems we face: they urge us to focus instead on structural inequality, antiblackness, and white supremacy at the core of schooling in the United States.[17] These two stances are not fundamentally opposed. Diversity is not magic; it is neither inherently good nor bad; it is a complicated, messy process with high-stakes outcomes. Making schools more diverse may increase children's access to valuable resources, yet all too often, it also centers the perspectives and priorities of White people. Families, educators, and policy makers may aspire to lofty goals as they advocate for diversity, but the outcomes are uncertain.

Education researchers and social scientists sometimes talk about the "hidden curriculum" of school—that is to say, the informal, implicit lessons about society and themselves that students learn alongside the explicit instruction they receive in academic subjects.[18] Like all hidden curricula, the lessons we learn from school diversity and integration are shaped not by our aspirations but by our everyday interactions. These unequal lessons are taught inside parent meetings, teachers' lounges, and classrooms as individuals enact education policies, policy discourses, and practices.

New York City Schools: Diverse and Segregated

The first time I read "Does the Negro Need Separate Schools?," I underlined this sentence, "To endure bad schools and wrong education because the schools are 'mixed' is a costly if not fatal mistake."[19] Du Bois called out the "public schools of Harlem" as a prime example of this problem: a nominally desegregated school system that served students very poorly. My years in New York City have shown me what he meant. As a child growing up in a White, wealthy suburb of the city, I had often visited New York, but I did not live there before 2009. Through my observations as an insider (current New Yorker, parent, educator) and an outsider (relative newcomer, not a classroom teacher), I have come to see New York City and its schools as both like and unlike many other parts of the country.

New York City's student demographics align neatly with how many people imagine "urban schools": 41 percent of New York City students are Latine, 24 percent are Black, 17 percent are Asian American, and 15 percent are White. Although many wealthy families live in the city, 72 percent of the students in New York City public schools are low income. Like many other urban school districts, the New York City Department of Education (NYCDOE) has focused on enrolling middle-class and professional families, who are typically but not always White, in the public school system. However, unlike many other cities, New Yorkers have also spent the past decade tensely and publicly debating whether and how to integrate our schools.

New York has both the largest and most segregated school system in the nation.[20] This has been the case for well over a century. In 1952, the city's schools were so intensely segregated that Ella Baker, then the director of the National Association for the Advancement of Colored People (NAACP) branch in New York City, made desegregation a primary focus of the civil rights organization's work. Two years later, in the wake of the *Brown* decision, Baker collaborated with the renowned social scientist and integration advocate Kenneth Clark to press for New York City school integration. In the decade that followed, parent activists pushed the protest further, refusing to send their children to substandard, segregated schools. Rather than making substantive changes, however, the New York City Board of Education convened a series of commissions and committees. That era's token efforts to address the city's systemic segregation included a voluntary transfer program that bused a grand total of thirteen Black students across Brooklyn for several hours each day.[21]

In 1964, over 460,000 students and teachers boycotted New York City schools to protest school segregation. This citywide boycott was the largest demonstration of the civil rights era, but it did not achieve its goal. White New Yorkers rallied in opposition to proposed busing initiatives and advocated for the segregated status quo under the banner of defending "neighborhood schools." Soon after, a Brooklyn Democrat helped insert language into the 1964 Civil Rights Act that ensured the legislation applied only to states (such as those in the South) that explicitly mandated segregated schools. While schools across the South were subject to federal desegregation orders under the Civil Rights Act, "racially unbalanced schools" in northern districts remained largely unaffected. Southern observers howled that the North willfully ignored the school segregation taking place in its own cities.[22]

During the 1970s, advocacy for school desegregation receded in the wake of massive "white flight" from New York City. A few decades later, however, the city began experiencing a wave of white return. Although city demographics changed, intense residential and school segregation persisted. In 2014, the UCLA Civil Rights Project denounced the New York City school system as one of the most segregated in the country—a status that has not changed in the following decade.[23] Even in gentrifying neighborhoods where the White population almost tripled between 2000 and 2016, schools remain highly segregated.[24] Seventy years after Ella Baker began her campaign against New York City school segregation, little has changed.

A Few Assumptions about Education Policy, Practice, and Research

I first learned about school diversity as an educator, next as a parent, and then as a researcher. Like other critical scholars, I recognize that my multiple experiences and identities inform the questions I ask, the data I collect, the analyses I conduct, and the meaning I make from my findings. I know that given my personal and professional standpoints, I am not an objective researcher or storyteller (as none of us is or ever could be). What is more, I have learned from critical race theorists that when educators, researchers, or policy makers claim neutrality, they often "camouflage the self-interest, power, and privilege of dominant groups in U.S. society."[25] One of my goals in this book is to unmask the roles that self-interest, power, and privilege continue to play in school diversity and integration.

I come to this work with three additional assumptions: that what matters most about educational policy is what people do with it; that what matters most about educational practice is what kids learn from it; and that racism is a systemic, rather than an individual, problem.

First, the question of what people do with policy. This book is, in many ways, about the limits of neoliberal approaches to education—that is to say, policies and policy discourses that aim to shift responsibility for public schools away from government and toward the marketplace.[26] I often find myself tempted to describe such approaches in broad terms, as if neoliberalism floats in the ether and gradually seeps down into schools and school systems. I try to resist this impulse. Instead, I strive to identify what the critical scholars Lois Weis and Michelle Fine call the "circuits of dispossession and privilege" that link "educational policy and everyday lives in schools."[27]

In order to reach this goal, I consider how people make and remake policy on the ground, through their daily practice. The education policy scholar Stephen Ball and his colleagues argue that teachers are "policy actors" who narrate, critique, advocate for, and otherwise play crucial roles in shaping educational policy.[28] These educators enact policy definition and implementation through their interactions with each other and their school contexts. I extend this line of thinking to consider how administrators, families, and—crucially—students also enact policy as they interact with each other, with educational systems, and with the social world. I build on Kate Phillippo's studies of students as policy actors, because I believe that understanding how students experience, perceive, and respond to policies in their schools and school systems can nuance our understanding of neoliberal approaches to education.[29] Whenever I have the opportunity, I approach young people as the subjects (rather than the objects) of educational policy. In particular, in chapters 2 and 3, I dive deep into how a few students experience diversifying schools. This approach builds on an extensive ethnographic tradition of using the experiences of individuals to illuminate broader social patterns.[30]

My focus on how kids think, feel, and act in racially diverse spaces is fundamentally related to the question of what students learn from school diversity. As the anthropologist of education Hugh Mehan argued three decades ago, "Schools are not black boxes through which students pass on their way.... They have a vibrant life composed of processes and practices that respond to competing demands that often unwittingly contribute to inequality."[31] Mehan points out that it is very challenging to figure out how those processes happen and what kids learn from them. For example, in the seven decades since the *Brown* decision, people have talked about how integration can influence student learning. However, we know surprisingly little about what happens inside diverse classrooms. I wanted to see what students and teachers *did*, as well as what they said, about school diversity. So I spent four years observing and talking with kindergartners, sixth graders, high school students, and the educators who worked with them in various diversifying settings. Before I began, I knew that to make sense of these observations and conversations, I would need to understand their social and political context. Therefore, before I collected data in schools, I spent two years watching school district meetings; interviewing administrators, families, and community members; examining policy documents; and combing through local media and social media archives related to school segregation and diversity.

Finally, there is the (enormous) question of racism. The sociologist Eve L. Ewing points out that many people think of racism as "something that lives in an individual" and is reflected in someone's actions and beliefs. Ewing compares this idea to the assumption that acting racist or antiracist is like riding a horse; it is a process in which a person makes a series of decisions about how to navigate a series of obstacles. However, she reminds us, many scholars and activists argue that racism is not actually an individual phenomenon. While it has important consequences for individuals, racism is better understood as a product of broader social systems and structures. Ewing therefore encourages us to see racism as riding a merry-go-round, rather than a horse: "you may be going up, down, and around, and you might feel like you're riding a horse, but the machine is functioning with or without you."[32] When considered from this point of view, what matters most is not whether people intend to be racist but how our adherence to established ways of doing things leads directly to racist outcomes.

This shift in perspective has important ramifications. For one, it means that pointing out racial patterns in schools is not the same as calling educators racist. Despite our long national tradition of blaming teachers for all our social problems, school staff are generally well-intentioned people who want to help kids.[33] Teachers are neither more nor less likely than other Americans to show racial bias.[34] However, like all of us, they operate in school and community contexts that are saturated with racial inequality. As they navigate their classrooms, schoolyards, and PTA meetings, they pull from available discourses to explain structural problems. Educators may point to kids' families or communities as the cause of their struggles; they may describe young children as "bad" or not trying hard enough; they may try to treat people the same, because they do not know how to address the fact that equal treatment does not generally lead to equal outcomes. These individuals may strive not to think racist thoughts, but they play a powerful role in a racist system—because that is the only system we have.

I have heard many people argue that integration and diversity are the best way to change this system. In chapter 3, you will meet one of these people: Principal Myers, who worked incredibly hard to build an integrated, antiracist school. After Principal Myers read the rough draft of this book, he told me that "antiracism is a verb." It is not something you are; it is something you do, and it is something you have to keep doing, all the time. This point of view both does and does not align with many popular conceptions of antiracism. For example, even though the historian Ibram X. Kendi writes that "racist and antiracist are not fixed identities," he also writes that the goal is to "be" antiracist.[35] Kendi's approach seems to move back and forth between approaching antiracism as an adjective and approaching it as a verb. Unlike Kendi, I am not sure it is possible for an individual to "be" antiracist. But I do know that it is possible for people to make antiracist choices. To extend Ewing's metaphor, I do not know whether we can ever jump off the merry-go-round. I am confident, however, that we can examine how the gears turn, acknowledge that we keep circling back to the same point, and work together to slow the machine down. These are imperfect actions we can and must take; in Principal Myers's words, they are verbs, not adjectives.

The Limits of School Diversity and Integration

This book examines what diversity and integration can and cannot offer our antiracist efforts, inside and outside schools. Is focusing on racial demographics, in Chancellor Banks's words, "playing around the margins"? My short (and probably frustrating) answer is, it depends. My research in diversifying schools and communities has taught me that common approaches to racial equity often reinscribe, rather than refute, deeply ingrained injustice. That does not mean that such efforts are pointless. It means that diversity, together with its close cousin integration, are best understood as strategies, rather than end goals. Advocates hope that making schools more diverse will also make them more racially just. However, *how* they pursue these goals and enact these strategies fundamentally affects their capacity to transform schools.

In order to look closely at various approaches to diversity and integration, each chapter in this book focuses on one educational space. I unpack these racial projects with clear eyes, weighing their affordances and constraints; in Diamond's words, I examine diverse learning environments "as they are, rather than as we wish they were."[36] Chapters 1 and 2 focus on the project of diversity, which gestures toward educational equity without directly addressing white supremacy. Chapter 1 shows how New York City district and school administrators make and remake neoliberal policy, constructing shared understandings of what diversity means and why it matters for schools and for students. This chapter centers on the question of who benefits from diversity, and I find that neoliberal policies lead administrators to prioritize recruiting and retaining White families in public schools. Chapter 2 examines the implications of this priority for kids. To illustrate the high stakes involved, I zoom in on the diverging experiences of two kindergarteners—a White girl and a Black boy—in one gentrifying elementary school.

Chapters 3 and 4 shift away from the project of diversity and toward the project of school integration, which uses educational policy and practice to directly intervene in racial inequality. These chapters closely examine two sites reaching toward what the legal scholar john a. powell calls "transformative" integration; they seek to counter neoliberal approaches by advocating for innovative policies and creating supportive learning environments for racially diverse learners.[37] Chapter 3 looks at how sixth graders experience the hidden curriculum of the antiracist middle school that Principal Myers led. We analyze the lessons that Michelle, a Black sixth grader, learned during her first year at her integrated school. Chapter 4 steps outside the formal education system, into a citywide, student-led campaign for school integration. We see what a group of racially diverse high school students did and did not learn about public policy and racial equity as they worked to change New York City high school admissions policies.

Taken as a whole, these four chapters look at how different people get caught up in diversity, how they navigate their entanglement, and what they learn from the process. Along the way, we see kids and adults playing multiple roles as they make and remake educational policy and practice. Researchers and educators already understand that diversity can be challenging; we already know that outcomes are often mixed. What we do not always recognize is the extent to which various approaches to diversity and integration are constructed by people on the ground. And all too often, we fail to examine how these crucial differences influence schools' central work: teaching and learning. After reading this book, I hope you will agree that if we want to make schools more just, the answer is neither to rely on the "magic" of integration nor to dismiss the material inequality exacerbated by segregation. Instead, we must recognize both the harms and the benefits that can come from diversity. We must address both the possibilities and the constraints of various approaches to shifting school demographics. And we must name the collective lessons we learn from the hidden curriculum of education policy and practice.

1

"We Weren't Special to Him"

Whiteness and Potential Diversity in New York City Schools

The District 41 conference room was getting crowded.¹ I pulled up a chair and looked around, counting heads: eighteen people squeezed around a large oval table in a warm, beige office space on a Thursday evening in May. From past meetings, I recognized school administrators, the district superintendent and his staff, NYCDOE community engagement representatives, members of the local Community Education Council (CEC), parents, and journalists with recorders placed strategically in the corner of the table. They all were here to learn how District 41 was preparing for recent changes to elementary school zone lines.

District 41, like many gentrifying areas in New York City, was both very diverse and very segregated. Some areas were filled with professional, primarily White, families who had been attracted by the district's parks, historic buildings, and easy access to public transit. Other areas of the district also featured tree-lined streets but were dominated by massive brick public housing complexes, first constructed in the 1950s, now serving almost exclusively Black and Latine families. It was easy for many residents to recognize a block, café, or playground as either "gentrified" or not. This was also true of the district's schools—including P.S. 411, the school under discussion that evening.

For decades, P.S. 411 had been known as the default destination for children who lived in nearby public housing. But in 2016, District 41 had worked with the NYCDOE office of student enrollment to redraw the boundaries of the school's catchment zone. This was not an unusual situation. District 41 was one of three New York City community school districts to rezone elementary schools in that year alone. In each of these controversial boundary changes, White middle-class and professional families who had previously been zoned to attend schools with families much like themselves were now assigned to schools that looked much like the rest of New York City: majority low income, majority Black and Latine. These changes sparked months of heated debate in each district before being approved.

That evening's rezoning meeting began with an update from the principal about changes at P.S. 411. For a long time, Principal Blake explained, the school's strengths had gone unnoticed by neighborhood newcomers. As the neighborhood gentrified, the school leadership team wanted to make sure that families who were new to the area could "familiarize themselves" with the school, its programs, and its philosophy. The principal enthusiastically described a redesign of P.S. 411's new website, thanking a parent volunteer for her leadership; the volunteer, a tall, blond, White woman who spoke with a French accent, smiled and nodded to the room. Optimistic projections for kindergarten enrollment soon followed. District Superintendent Arnett nodded along as he listened, then reassured the room that the zone changes would not result in "winners and losers," since all the "kids have the opportunity to go to a great school."

After a pause, Kimani, a Black man whose daughter was enrolled at P.S. 411, cleared his throat and declared, "I love all the good stuff. I love all the beautiful. Now let's talk about the bad and the ugly. And I think that is where the real work begins." Kimani's six-year-old daughter, sitting beside him in a pink sweatshirt and Afro puffs, looked up from her iPad and took off her headphones to listen to her father. Kimani looked around the table and announced, "There are weeds in the garden that we need to address." He explained, P.S. 411 "is what you would call an inner-city school, right?" And he knew there was a "negative connotation" associated with any school serving African American and Latine students. However, Kimani charged, resistance to enrollment changes at P.S. 411 was just one small part of a broader educational "epidemic":

"The most segregated state is New York, in the country. The most segregated district is New York City. We're not talking about South Carolina flying Confederate flags here. We're talking about New York City. That's supposed to be the melting pot for immigrants, African Americans, and Latinos. And I know that's a conversation that a lot of us don't want to have, but that is a real conversation." Kimani spoke for over five minutes, detailing his concerns about the "issue of the privileged" people who refused to send their children to schools with majority Black and Latine students. He denounced the ways the NYCDOE systematically silenced the concerns of Black and Latine families, detailed the ways in which these families were marginalized in public schools, and lamented the resulting lack of trust between NYCDOE staff and the families they served. As he spoke, Superintendent Arnett and Principal Blake, who are also Black, gazed silently out the conference room window. Their expressions were carefully blank.

Kimani argued that cheerful talk about welcoming neighborhood newcomers was a problem: "I don't want us to be in a state where we're making P.S. 411 comfortable for the affluent White people coming in." Principal Blake drew in her breath sharply at those words, saying, "So—" but then stopped short, biting her lower lip and writing down a note on a legal pad. Kimani did not appear to notice. He gestured toward his daughter, saying, "I fear the day that I have to tell this little girl, right here, that she cannot do something because of the color of her skin. I refuse to let her friend, who's White, have anyone tell me that this little White boy, who is the only White boy in his classroom, is getting an inferior education. . . . If your child is the only White kid in these classrooms, then your child is not getting an inferior education. Your child is getting a superior education." Kimani argued that P.S. 411 did not need these new students to be "a great school." What it needed was to change families' assumptions.

Superintendent Arnett was ready to respond. After clarifying some specifics about district policies, he circled back to Kimani's larger point: "I think that the things that you raised are huge issues for this city, for this state, and for this country, quite frankly. Right? But how can we make an impact in the garden in which we are tilling? . . . If we could not get a rezoning done in a way that was respectful and that people came out on the other side not bloodied and battered—what would be the hope for Omaha, Nebraska, if in this city, we could not get that work done?" With that question hanging in the air, a representative from the NYCDOE office for community engagement jumped into the conversation, reminding the crowded room that P.S. 411 was not the only school in the city facing demographic changes. There was an integration committee working with the district, "and the increasing diversity is really exciting": "I'm really only saying that the neighborhood schools are more inclusive, but more representative of their neighborhoods, and I think that P.S. 411 is a great neighborhood school." Superintendent Arnett agreed: "We're in the infancy of this work and by no means have gotten it right all the time. But I do think it has opened up huge conversations in this district that are being looked at citywide and nationally."

As I listened to this interchange, I scribbled a rapidly growing list of phrases in the margins of my notebook: "great schools," "inner-city schools," "neighborhood schools," "segregated schools," "diverse schools." I considered the various ways I had heard people describe different schools, families, and neighborhoods in this gentrifying school district. Whom do these conversations serve? What assumptions do they include about diversity, segregation, and what makes a "proper education"? What role do the priorities and preferences of White families play in our responses to these questions?

I answer these questions by examining the hidden curriculum of school diversity—the ways that policies and policy discourses not only reflect but also reinforce deeply rooted assumptions about public school students, their families, and their communities. While educators and education researchers frequently refer to the hidden curriculum of schooling, they often fail to recognize that educational policy also has a hidden curriculum. Policy is pedagogical: we learn from the options it does and does not make available, as well as from conversations like the one that Kimani, Principal Blake, and Superintendent Arnett had that evening. This learning has important consequences for students, educators, and communities.

Early in my fieldwork, I sat in a District 41 diversity committee meeting with Nadine, a Black mother and an educator who told a story about her own child's school. Nadine had transferred her son to an elementary school on the other side of the district because she believed he would receive a better education there than in the one he was zoned to attend. Like the school in Nadine's neighborhood, this school was majority Black, but it was beginning to enroll a few White and professional families. Nadine had heard her child's principal talk about getting even more "special people" to attend their school. She told the diversity committee that his comments "sickened" her, because it seemed very clear to Nadine that "we weren't special to him." While this principal was unusually direct about how he considered certain families more special than others, his attitude was not unusual. As the sociologist Maia Cucchiara explains, many urban school districts approach White and middle-class families as "highly valued customers" who are "inherently more worthy and important" than others.[2]

Superintendent Arnett, Principal Blake, and other District 41 leaders would never have wanted to send Nadine or any other parent the message that they were not highly valued. However, they were grasping for responses to the challenge Kimani articulated: "What strategies are we going to do to make sure that we have a fair, integrated system?" This chapter tells the story of how district administrators like Superintendent Arnett, school leaders like Principal Blake, and parents like Nadine and Kimani coconstruct the hidden curriculum of school diversity. In order to understand this story, we will first examine how the landscape of neoliberal policy approaches and diversity advocacy in New York City shaped the options available to District 41 administrators. Then we will see how district staff rebranded their schools as *potentially* diverse, despite the district's extreme racial and socioeconomic stratification. With the support of the NYCDOE, school and district leaders marketed public schools to the people they saw as capable of realizing this potential diversity: primarily White, professional families. Ironically, their urgent desire to increase low-income Black and Latine students' access to educational resources prompted them to center whiteness. Along the way, these policy actors unintentionally exacerbated the racial inequality they strove to interrupt.

Neoliberal Policy and the School Marketplace

New York City school enrollment policies are both like and unlike those of many other cities in the United States. In 2002, the city's system of over eighteen hundred schools, serving almost one million students, was placed under the control of Mayor Michael Bloomberg. While thirty-two "community school districts" (like District 41) administer and support local elementary and middle schools, New York has no elected school boards and offers very limited opportunities for families and communities to influence educational policy. In the early 2000s, Bloomberg's schools chancellor, Joel Klein, used mayoral control to initiate a series of systemwide reforms. He closed schools labeled "underperforming" and dramatically expanded the school choice system. Although controversial, these actions reflected the bipartisan consensus of that era of school reform. No Child Left Behind, the George W. Bush administration's 2001 reauthorization of the federal Elementary and Secondary Education Act, similarly focused on holding schools and educators "accountable." In New York City and across the nation, standardized test data were closely examined for differences in student achievement based on race or ethnicity, income, English proficiency, and special education status. School districts were required to make these data public and to offer families ways to "opt out" of "low-performing schools."[3] Bloomberg and Klein's reforms reflected these trends, reshaping the city's educational policies according to the values of choice, competition, and accountability.

These reforms reflect the logics of neoliberalism: the belief that, as the political scientist Cathy Cohen writes, the market is better than the state at producing outcomes that are "fair, sensible, and good for all." These policies are bolstered by public discourse that "emphasizes personal responsibility and the role of individual agency or choice in determining one's success."[4] The educational policy scholar Pauline Lipman argues that neoliberal approaches not only fundamentally shift school and district governance structures—although they certainly do that. They also "reconstruct values, social relations, and social identities," creating a new social imaginary in which public school students and their families are consumers of services, rather than citizens with rights.[5] However, neoliberal approaches do more than position citizens as consumers. They also demand that the public employees tasked with implementing education policies take on the role of salespeople. Neoliberal approaches hold the city, state, and federal policy responsible for keeping schools accountable and for offering a range of enrollment choices; they hold school and district administrators responsible for marketing schools; and they hold families responsible for making informed decisions that benefit their own children. They hold the marketplace—that is to say, nobody in particular—responsible for attending to the public good.

Advantaging the Advantaged: School Choice and Segregation in New York City

Many New Yorkers are deeply uncomfortable with the fact that New York City schools are extremely segregated. In 2014, Gary Orfield, a nationally renowned scholar of school segregation at the UCLA Civil Rights Project, called New York the "epicenter of educational segregation in the nation."[6] Policy makers, educators, and families who often imagined themselves leaders in the fight for racial justice were dismayed to hear that their city lagged behind most of the country. Like Superintendent Arnett, these advocates asked themselves, "What would be the hope for Omaha, Nebraska, if in this city, we could not get that work done?"

School diversity advocates worried about an increasingly evident citywide pattern: due to an influx of White and professional families into gentrifying neighborhoods, areas like District 41 were considerably more racially and economically diverse than the rest of the city but their local schools did not reflect this diversity.[7] Although gentrification had decreased residential segregation in some parts of the city, close to 50 percent of White students who lived in gentrifying communities attended schools outside their own neighborhoods.[8] Even in neighborhoods where the White population had almost tripled between 2000 and 2016, schools remained highly segregated.[9] In a foreword to a Civil Rights Project report that Orfield coauthored with John Kucsera about New York City school segregation, Orfield asked, "What are we doing to bring the newcomer families into the neighborhood schools, where they will demand and support schools that prepare their children, and the children of families already there, for college?"[10] New York City policy makers and education leaders, like their counterparts in Philadelphia, the Bay Area, Washington, DC, and other cities, often asked themselves the same question, dedicating considerable resources to recruiting and retaining White and professional families in locally zoned public schools.[11]

Choice-based enrollment policies have played a central role in many efforts to create diverse schools, despite overwhelming evidence that school choice increases segregation.[12] In New York City, admissions to elementary and middle schools are centralized and managed by the NYCDOE. A labyrinthine student enrollment system assigns each incoming kindergartener a zone for a nearby elementary school on the basis of their address. However, families can also choose to enter a lottery for seats in kindergarten classrooms outside their zoned school, including other zoned schools within their community school district, unzoned district schools, or special dual-language bilingual programs. Some four-year-olds may also be eligible for admission to specialized district or citywide Gifted and Talented programs. Students are assigned to schools by the city's central NYCDOE lottery system via an algorithm based on an array of factors, such as residential address and sibling enrollment.[13]

School choice policies serve many advantaged families quite well. Some wealthy New Yorkers strategically opt to buy (or rent second apartments) in expensive real estate markets with "high-performing" local elementary schools. Others, including many middle-class and professional parents, devote considerable time, savvy, and resources to navigating the choice process for schools outside their local zone. These families spend several months attending school tours, paying for "educational consultants," parsing publicly accessible data, and discussing their lottery rankings with other families like themselves on the playground.[14] They invest heavily in this process, because they are acutely aware that elementary school placement has long-term consequences for New York City students. Highly regarded middle schools draw heavily from certain elementary schools, and matriculation from these selective middle schools will, in turn, dramatically increase students' chances of acceptance at the city's most selective high schools. By rewarding families who are best positioned to devote time, effort, and money to the school choice process, New York City's enrollment policies play a central role in the city's highly stratified, extremely segregated educational landscape.

Diverse Schools as Urban Amenities

Joel Klein, Mayor Bloomberg's schools chancellor, considered school integration an anachronistic goal; he believed in holding all schools accountable to high standards, rather than moving students around between schools. The 2012 election of Mayor Bill de Blasio, who was considerably to Bloomberg's left, raised advocates' hopes that school desegregation would become a priority for the NYCDOE. However, very little changed.

Mayor de Blasio saw student enrollment policy as crucial to one of the city's central goals: urban development. The de Blasio administration, like the Bloomberg administration, saw gentrification—the economic and social processes that enable private capital and individuals to invest in and change previously neglected neighborhoods and cities—as a form of urban renewal.[15] As Cucchiara argues, this view leads urban school districts not only to approach White middle-class and professional families as valued customers but also to approach public schools as assets to be managed in the residential and educational marketplaces.[16]

Both policy makers and affluent families in New York City are highly aware of the tight relationship between schools and property values. When the NYCDOE proposed school rezonings, local media inevitably broadcast the voices of outraged parents whose children would be affected by the new zone lines. In three rezoning debates in 2016 alone, news reports quoted parents fuming, "It'll take thousands, maybe a hundred thousand dollars off the value of my apartment. . . . We moved here for that school, and that school is kind of our right."[17] Mayor de Blasio considered these concerns valid and important. When a reporter asked the mayor why the city could not do more to promote school integration, de Blasio replied that you have to "respect" families who "made massive life decisions and investments because of which school their kid would go to."[18] Countless public meetings were dedicated to tweaks to school zone lines and school admissions policies. The NYCDOE spent a great deal of time and effort addressing the concerns of families who had counted on residential addresses and student assignment policies to ensure access to specific schools. The vast majority of these families were White; many appeared to consider a seat in their preferred elementary school, like their real estate investments, part of their personal property.[19]

At times, the connection between school policy and urban development goals was made quite explicit. Carmen Fariña, who served as schools chancellor for most of Mayor de Blasio's term, was the architect of his administration's educational policy. Fariña was committed to undoing many Bloomberg-era accountability reforms. However, she simultaneously embraced gentrification and school choice as viable strategies for school improvement. At a 2016 town hall in Bedford-Stuyvesant—a historic Black Brooklyn power center that was rapidly gentrifying by the time de Blasio took office—Fariña responded to a question about school segregation in gentrifying communities: "One thing I've recommended to superintendents is, have breakfast with your real estate agent, particularly the real-estate agents in the new developments going up."[20] Fariña repeatedly encouraged superintendents to market local schools to the affluent families buying real estate in gentrifying neighborhoods. At a 2017 district town hall, the chancellor explained to an auditorium full of parents, educators, and district representatives, "One of the suggestions I made, is that you're going to rebrand. And your neighborhood is changing. How do we get the parents who don't even think they're going to be into our schools, into them?"[21] Like many other neoliberal policy makers, Fariña saw marketing schools as a route to educational equity.

The sociologists Maia Cucchiara, Linn Posey-Maddox, and Hava Rachel Gordon have convincingly shown that it is common for cities to treat public schools as urban amenities and to approach gentrifiers as valued customers.[22] What distinguishes the intersection of gentrification and school choice in New York is that the city frequently uses *diversity* to market its schools. In District 41, NYCDOE staff, district administrators, and school leaders used what Joyce Bell and Douglas Hartmann call the "happy talk" of diversity to tailor choice policy and marketing messages.[23] As the education policy scholar Erica Turner argues, these marketing decisions are structured by policy makers' and administrators' tacit recognition that the choice-based market for public schools is always highly racialized and that White middle-class and professional families are the target audience.[24]

NYCDOE and District 41 staff signaled to gentrifiers that local schools had the potential to become, in the sociologist Ellen Berrey's terms, "model diverse communities."[25] In order to help primarily White, professional families feel welcome in "neighborhood schools," these administrators explicitly appealed to gentrifiers' priorities, tastes, and values. For example, during another P.S. 411 rezoning meeting, a NYCDOE spokesperson explained that the Department of Education hoped to create "a community school, . . . a school where everybody in the neighborhood who chooses a school can be part of that school": "I think that school choice is something that sometimes we talk about as something of the Bloomberg administration, but certainly we want parents to send their kids to schools that they *want* to send their kids to." She went on to describe what she considered "the elephant in the room": District 41 was working to "increase diversity" so that schools are not only more inclusive but also "more representative of their [gentrifying] neighborhoods."

These comments reflected a fundamental reality of educational policy in New York City. Although the de Blasio administration used more progressive language than the Bloomberg administration did, there were very few differences in the two administrations' stances on school segregation and school choice. NYCDOE policy makers and district staff continued to approach the public school system as a choice-based marketplace. They simply added "diversity" to the list of market values.

"We Do Not Share a Language": Defining and Not Defining School Diversity

In the wake of the *Brown* decision, the New York City Board of Education had described its school system as "separated" rather than "segregated." Sixty years later, the de Blasio administration preferred similarly vague language. Segregation, an established policy problem, demanded policy responses—interventions such as busing, which White, middle-class New Yorkers had long resisted.[26] Instead, the de Blasio administration suggested diversity and token actions similar to those the city had long used with little impact. When Chancellor Fariña was asked how the city could address school segregation, she suggested setting up a "sister schools" program with pen pals who "visit each other on different occasions and understand that they live in different neighborhoods, but they're basically the same kind of kids," an idea surprisingly similar to a school intervisitation program established by the Board of Education in 1954, which paired pen pals from Black and White schools.[27] The Board of Education had assembled a series of task forces in response to public outcry about school segregation in the

1960s; the de Blasio administration also convened multiple committees to study the issue, while taking very little action. In 2016, as public pressure to change student enrollment policies increased, Chancellor Fariña explained, "I want to see diversity in schools organically. I don't want to see mandates."[28] Unlike integration, "organic" diversity has the benefit of being marketable.

Yet, at times, it was unclear exactly what the New York City Department of Education even meant by "diverse." Indeed, the School Diversity Advisory Group (SDAG), which was made up of NYCDOE representatives, parents, educators, students, and scholars, acknowledged in its official report, "we do not, as a group or a city, share a language to talk about issues of diversity, inclusion, integration, and equity." The SDAG went on to claim that they "embrace the values these words embody," while never specifying precisely what those terms meant.[29] By 2024, the official NYCDOE webpage about "diversity in our schools" included "racial background" as one item on a long list of ways schools could be diverse, along with other categories such as "home language," "ability," "religion," "gender identity," and "lived experience."[30] The NYCDOE thus engaged in what the ethnic studies scholar Jodi Melamed calls "official antiracism" that renders race merely one of several "cultural" factors, making attempts to address structural inequality appear less important or unfair.[31] In these official policy discourses, the precise nature of "diversity" is unclear, and its power lies in experiencing difference, rather than in addressing structural inequality. The central role that race plays in our educational processes, systems, and outcomes remains unacknowledged, even as advocates and policy makers embrace "diverse schools."

In the rare moments when the NYCDOE did respond to accusations of school segregation, the problem was generally framed as socioeconomic. In some ways, this could be understood as a tactical decision. In the landmark 2007 *PICS v. Seattle* Supreme Court decision on school desegregation programs, Chief Justice John Roberts famously wrote that "the way to stop discrimination on the basis of race is to stop discriminating on the basis of race."[32] The *PICS* decision therefore severely restricted—although it did not completely eliminate—the conditions under which school districts could consider race in student assignment. As a result, when the NYCDOE took small steps to support school diversity, these initiatives almost always relied on socioeconomic criteria. In 2015, the city eagerly participated in a New York State pilot program that incentivized districts to develop and market "cutting-edge academic programs" in low-performing schools in order to "attract higher SES [socioeconomic status] students."[33] A year later, the NYCDOE initiated a "diversity in admissions" pilot program that allowed schools to create "priority groups" for student admissions. Most of these schools had long served low-income Black and Latine children, but their principals worried that school demographics were "tipping" toward White students as neighborhoods gentrified. The most common factors prioritized in the diversity in admissions program were socioeconomic, such as eligibility for free or reduced-price lunch or families in temporary housing. In other words, even when the NYCDOE was willing to interrupt the segregated status quo, it did so in the name of socioeconomic, rather than racial, diversity.

Diversity advocates such as Orfield often argue that "a half century of research shows that middle class children's test scores are not harmed by integration while the scores of Black and Latino children generally increase."[34] This argument relies on several implicit assumptions: that race and class labels can be used interchangeably; that test scores are an accurate representation of school quality; and that low-income children of color are the primary beneficiaries of diverse schools. These assumptions form the backbone of the hidden curriculum of school diversity.

How Diversity Embraces Deficit-Based Approaches

Ironically, diversity policies and policy discourses often avoid talking directly about race. Administrators and policy makers frequently rely on coded, color-evasive language to market diverse schools as urban amenities, refer vaguely to the undefined value of diversity, or rely on exclusively socioeconomic frameworks to address inequality.[35] However, as Ewing writes, "race has a way of filling space even as it remains invisible."[36] If we do not examine how race informs our interpretations and our interactions, we cannot address the role that it plays in educational policy and within schools. Instead, we attribute systemic policy decisions to market failures, bad individual choices, and the collective deficits of students, families, and the educators who serve them.[37]

In fact, deficit-based approaches are at the heart of neoliberal diversity policy and discourse. The sociologist Amy Stuart Wells argues that regardless of the support that low-income communities of color offer each other and the excellent work that teachers often do with children in these communities, their neighborhoods and schools "are rarely, if ever, deemed to be highly reputable or even 'good.'"[38] Instead, school reputations draw on deficit-based racial and socioeconomic stereotypes. Schools serving low-income kids of color are called "segregated," a label with distinctly negative connotations. (What is more, it is a label that schools serving almost exclusively White and affluent communities generally avoid, despite the fact that these schools are also extremely segregated.) The assumption that such schools and the children who attend them are inferior is fundamental to the case that many administrators and policy makers make for school diversity.

Many White, middle-class, and professional New Yorkers are skeptical that schools serving primarily low-income Black, Latine, and immigrant children—that is to say, the overwhelming majority of New York City public school students—could be considered "good." Indeed, the families who did not want their children rezoned to P.S. 411 publicly detailed their anxieties: the school was not safe, its curriculum was lacking, and teachers would need to be "retrained" in order to work effectively with their own, more advantaged children. What is more, these parents vividly described their concerns about the presumed deficits of the school's student body. One caller to a public radio show explained his fears about sending his son to a rezoned school: "We are afraid that the kids around him wouldn't be as prepared as his classmates are now. . . . I think moving other children to that school by the projects will probably raise the children already in that school to a higher bar. But that's not what we bargained for when we chose this school zone." Perhaps unsurprisingly, this father believed his child would contribute assets to the school and the low-income Black and Brown children who attended it—whom he presumed to be inferior—but his own family would gain little in return.

Like many others, this parent judged schools and children based on their demographics. Such comments made explicit the often-unspoken assumptions about which students offer value to a school, community, or classroom. During the White backlash against school segregation in the 1960s, calls for "neighborhood schools" were an expression of resistance to busing and other integration policies. Fifty years later, however, the designation "diverse neighborhood school" now denotes the presence of what Posey-Maddox calls a "critical mass" of White, middle-class or professional families.[39] Families, educators, and local policy makers often believe that without this substantive White presence, a school cannot succeed.[40] As one self-identified urban, progressive, and White mother told Shani Evans, "I wanted diversity, but not so much."[41] Such parents consider White middle-class and professional families a much-needed counterbalance to the presumed pathology of segregated schools. In the words of that public radio caller, they understand school diversity as a way to bring low-income children and children of color up to "a higher bar"—potentially lowering the bar for their own children. These families, along with many educators and policy makers, consider the students who attend segregated schools a problem, in and of themselves. Many diversity advocates therefore see White, professional families as a way to balance or fix a school with too many of "those" kids.

Rebranding District 41: "The Weight and Heaviness of What We're Trying to Do"

The 2014 Civil Rights Project report identifying New York as one of the most segregated school systems in the country posed a significant marketing challenge for the city. There was a public consensus that nobody wanted to send their kids to segregated schools, especially in a progressive place like New York. However, that consensus was accompanied by an assumption that significant changes to enrollment policies would never be politically viable—as the mayor had explicitly stated, city policies must "respect" families who had invested in sending their children to specific schools. What is more, the de Blasio administration rarely acknowledged a central challenge involved in "organically" diversifying New York City schools: in a city where less than 15 percent of students are White and over 73 percent of students live in poverty, it is difficult to make the numbers work. Few public schools would be considered palatable options by the city's most valued customers, in large part because they lacked a critical mass of families like themselves to go around.

Nonetheless, district staff and school leaders were tasked with marketing school diversity to gentrifying communities. In District 41, the superintendent and her staff took this responsibility seriously, as did Principal Blake of P.S. 411. Like the de Blasio administration, these district leaders often focused on appealing to the families they saw as special. They rebranded schools that served primarily low-income Black and Latine children as *potentially* diverse—if only White, affluent families would choose to attend them. However, both school and district administrators struggled with tensions between their goal of marketing diverse schools and the limits of choice-based policies. As they navigated this contested terrain in district town halls, PTA meetings, and local media, they made and remade school diversity policy on the ground.

Superintendent Arnett was not afraid to name the linked challenges of residential and school segregation. During the years I spent in District 41, I repeatedly heard staff refer to the district's "haves and have-nots."

Indeed, Superintendent Arnett and his staff often described the district's challenges as "a tale of two cities." District 41 was changing; while part of the district had long been affluent and another part had long been poor, gentrification had shifted demographic patterns. In the past five years, there was an increase from 8 percent to 15 percent of White students in District 41. Only 41 percent of students in the district were now Black; 27 percent were Latine; and 17 percent were Asian American. At the same time, the percentage of poor students attending District 41 schools had decreased from 79 percent to 70 percent. In district leadership team meetings, Superintendent Arnett frequently reminded his staff that they were "in the fishbowl" facing "the hot-button issues of race, class, and academic excellence" that districts across the city and the country faced.

Like the chancellor and the mayor, the superintendent considered it his job to address the priorities of the district's shifting population. The district hosted a series of community meetings related to school assignment policies. The first event was held in an elementary school library; people sat at tables clustered in the middle of the room, surrounded by bookshelves filled with picture books. I shared a table with a White kindergarten teacher, a Black father of a fourth grader, a White mother of a first grader, and a White mother of a fifth grader. We listened to Superintendent Arnett's welcome address, which described the "impact of housing on who goes to our schools," "high rents," and "rapid gentrification." The superintendent argued that these neighborhood changes were closely linked to changes in what people "need, want, and desire" from public schools. Then our table worked as a group to identify our shared criteria for what Du Bois had called a "proper education," prioritizing characteristics from a list that included items like "diverse student body," "quality arts programs," and "high standardized test scores." This was information the district needed to achieve the superintendent's goal: "all our schools will be great schools and attractive to the wide range of families in the district."

Like many gentrifying areas, District 41 included a few schools that were in high demand, were crowded for space, and enrolled significant numbers of affluent White families. Most district schools, however, were underenrolled, struggled for resources, and were attended almost exclusively by low-income Black and Latine children. District 41 staff were deeply concerned with the well-being of these students, their communities, and their schools; they saw increasing student enrollment as the most viable path to increased school funding. Since many gentrifying families sent their children to schools outside the district, these neighborhood newcomers were the focus of much of the district's recruitment and retention efforts. District 41, like the NYCDOE, was highly responsive to these families' priorities and accommodated their preferences. For example, the district expanded the number of dual-language bilingual classrooms in response to interest from English-speaking families who wanted their children to learn a second language. This local decision reflected citywide trends; as Kate Menken and her colleagues demonstrate, NYCDOE has increasingly leveraged dual-language immersion programs "to re-engineer their school's demographics by bringing in more White and otherwise privileged students."[42]

Superintendent Arnett and his staff believed that although some schools in the district needed to make programmatic changes, many others simply needed to improve their reputations. In leadership team meetings, administrators discussed the importance of "clarifying misconceptions" about certain schools and opening them up to the public, because "seeing is believing." Staff told me that while some elementary schools had become "more marketable and more chic," many others had not. In response, the district hired a corporate management consultant who drafted a District 41 vision statement. The draft, titled "A District Re-imagined for All," included headings such as "Collaboration," "Equity," and "Options." However, the longest section by far was titled "Rebranding." It opened with the statement, "It shouldn't surprise you that our district opens every school to rebranding," then continued that "in this re-imagined district . . . you see schools that have taken the time and the energy and the resources large and small to rebrand themselves." Diversity played a central role in this work: the district's new website prominently featured the efforts of the diversity committee, the expansion of dual-language immersion programs, and middle-school choice options.

Superintendent Arnett took great pride in the district's progress. He told his staff that Chancellor Fariña had called their efforts "important," explaining that the chancellor believed that "schools should be diverse." Indeed, Superintendent Arnett reported with a smile during one district leadership team meeting, the chancellor had dubbed him "the diversity king." His staff enthusiastically embraced this nickname.

Like the mayor and the chancellor, District 41 leadership avoided the word "integration." Shonda, a Black staff member who handled district-wide budgeting processes, told me that integration was a "fad." She considered absurd the idea that any one school was "going to swing a complete pendulum" as a result of diversity initiatives. Instead, the district was going to offer families a "portfolio" of schools diverse in culture, race, academic performance, and programming. In Berrey's words, Shonda and her colleagues gave "new meaning to the racial order" by framing diversity as "a social good and a competitive advantage, to be honored and appropriately managed."[43]

At the same time, district staff were clearly mindful of the potential costs of diversity initiatives. Annie, who was also Black, led district-wide family engagement initiatives. She had herself been bused as a child to a middle school across the city; she shared vivid memories of her mother's "concern about [her] being the only child of color going to school, with good reason," since "people in that community overturned a city bus with children on it because they were angry" about busing mandates ten years prior. Annie and Shonda understood longtime District 41 residents' concerns that diversity initiatives were another form of gentrification. They listened carefully when an African American woman in one town hall asked, "Are we doing this for *them* or because it's the right thing to do?" Shonda told me she was very worried by people she heard "on both sides" who argued that the only way schools would improve was if more

White students attended them. These comments contributed to Shonda's fundamental concern that marketing school diversity might reinforce assumptions that "Black is dumb, White is smart." Like her colleagues in the district offices, she appeared at times to struggle with what she called "the weight and heaviness of what we're trying to do."

However, District 41 staff had few options. The schools they supported were required to maintain student enrollment in order to access much-needed "per pupil" funds. The de Blasio administration had made clear that marketing schools, rather than mandating integration, was the clearest path to achieving NYCDOE enrollment targets. What is more, as Turner points out, district administrators have a vested interest in reaching these goals: their "legitimacy, authority, and jobs depended upon sustaining the school systems that they led and presenting themselves as professionals with solutions to pressing problems."[44] Turner argues that managing diversity is a central part of this work.[45] These public employees may not have wanted to affirm the existing racial order, but they needed to address the priorities and desires of newcomers to District 41.

"Like an Oreo Cookie": Selling Potential Diversity at P.S. 411

A year after P.S. 411 had been rezoned, Principal Blake described a picnic she had held to welcome incoming pre-K and kindergartener families to their new school. She told me with a smile, "It was fifty-fifty. It looked like an Oreo cookie, literally. You had 50 percent Black/Latino, 50 percent Caucasian. And ideally, I'd like to keep it that way. . . . I wish I could freeze that." Principal Blake knew, however, that maintaining those demographics would be challenging and not entirely up to her. If the P.S. 411 attendance zone further gentrified, demographics might shift in one direction. And if Principal Blake could not convince gentrifiers to send their children to P.S. 411, her school would never be diverse at all.

While District 41 staff oversaw district-wide rebranding efforts, the work of convincing families to choose individual schools was left largely to school leaders. Superintendent Arnett was quite direct in communicating this responsibility to principals. In a leadership team meeting, he told district staff that he had urged one principal in a gentrifying neighborhood to pay attention to the three cranes outside his window, asking, "What are you doing to engage new families in the district?" In contrast, the superintendent did not have to remind the principal of P.S. 411 about the importance of reaching out to gentrifiers. Due to the rezoning debates, Principal Blake was already paying close attention.

When I asked Principal Blake how she felt about P.S. 411's changing student body, she sighed and told me, "I don't have much control over what happens in the neighborhood as far as construction and gentrification and development. I have absolutely no control over that, right?" Principal Blake continued with a shrug, "So the neighborhood will change as it changes, and obviously with that, the face of the school might change a little bit. And I'm very realistic, and I can probably predict what it will look like in five years from now. It'll look very different than it does now." She had to put aside her feelings of being "saddened by the change in the community" or any harsh words that had been shared during the controversial school rezoning, because she saw her job as moving students "academically and social-emotionally" and "promot[ing] diversity." She said, almost defiantly, "All I can do is control what happens within these walls."

Principal Blake told me with a nervous chuckle, "I just want to be a principal!" However, as Superintendent Arnett had made clear, a significant portion of the principal's job involved convincing neighborhood newcomers to send their children to her school. Principal Blake considered her own opinions about gentrification, student enrollment, and city policies irrelevant. Recruiting and retaining new families was crucial to her professional success. If a school did not have enough students, it would lose funding; if things got bad enough, the school might close.

Principal Blake, like many people in the community, was highly aware that her capacity to recruit new families was affected by her school's student demographics. Susan, a White woman who volunteered at P.S. 411, explained that during the rezoning debates, White parents were "making outright claims about that school being of poor quality or being dangerous or this and that, without any nuance, depth of real knowledge—just hearsay, also taking one stripe of a piece of information and blowing it up to represent the whole school. Whether they meant it or not, sounding incredibly racist and ignorant." Susan paused, then repeated slowly, "I think there was *some* racism and a *lot* of ignorance." Like District 41 staff, she believed that the only way to address racist ignorance was to encourage neighborhood newcomers to see the school for themselves. Susan explained that she herself would have been very happy to send her son to P.S. 411 because she had been so impressed in the time she spent there. However, it did not matter how great P.S. 411 was if other people did not recognize it.

Principal Blake eagerly welcomed newcomers to P.S. 411. The school leadership team developed a series of "P.S. 411 and Me" workshops featuring fun activities for parents and toddlers. Laughing nervously and insisting that the design was not her idea, she showed district administrators a flier featuring a cartoon image of a Black princess labeled "Principal Blake," dazzling small children with her magic wand. The flier's playful imagery, emphasis on hands-on activities, and welcoming language communicated that neighborhood newcomers would feel comfortable at an otherwise unfamiliar school. District 41 staff loved the idea. In Annie's words, these marketing events were an "awesome opportunity for parents just to get to know the school as a place they may want to bring their children." And that was the district's primary goal.

Superintendent Arnett, dedicated to supporting P.S. 411's rezoning, praised Principal Blake's efforts in district leadership team meetings. He explained that he was also working with NYCDOE offices to upgrade P.S. 411's physical plant, in recognition of "all the newness going on at the school." As I listened, I wondered if the superintendent was similarly engaged at other district schools that lacked this "newness" and potential diversity. I wondered if those school facilities were receiving the upgrades they needed. I also noted the time, effort, and resources that school and district leaders had devoted to making P.S. 411 feel welcoming for newcomers, which must have affected the support they could offer other schools.

I spent much of the following school year at P.S. 411, where I saw even more evidence of the central role that school marketing occupied in administrative time, effort, and resources. Like many New York City schools, P.S. 411 hosted weekly tours throughout the fall for families who were weighing their prekindergarten and kindergarten options. The overwhelming majority of parents attending tours of P.S. 411 appeared to be White, wore professional dress, brought babies in expensive carriers or strollers, and had other markers the neighborhood commonly associated with newcomers.

As I observed one school tour, I remembered Annie from District 41 saying, "Parents who are more educated have different expectations. . . . If I walked into a school and I have my son, who is attending preschool, and I'm looking for a school for him, I'm looking for certain things. I'm in demand for those things. If I don't see it, I'm turning around, and I'm going to the next place and looking for that." Ms. Diana, the lower-grades assistant principal, seemed to anticipate these demands. The beginning of the tour took place in the school cafeteria, with parents sitting in rows at long lunchroom tables. Ms. Diana opened with a slide show featuring the school's academic programs, community partnerships, small class sizes, and rich resources. She went on to talk about all the ways that P.S. 411 welcomes families, such as encouraging parents to drop off children in the classroom rather than the schoolyard, so they can get a sense of what happens during the school day. Ms. Diana enthusiastically described the school's "active PTA" and social media presence, emphasizing how easy it is to get updates about what is going on through Facebook, Instagram, and the school website. Parents raised their hands as soon as she finished her presentation, asking questions about special programs, STEM (science, technology, engineering, and mathematics) instruction, and recess time. Principal Blake jumped in, detailing her school's many resources and emphasizing that P.S. 411 is a "school of choice." She and Ms. Diana described their "high expectations" for students and teachers and efforts to help children and families feel "ownership" of the classroom, school, and community. Parents nodded along, apparently liking the idea of a school where they belonged and that belonged to them.

Some teachers, however, worried that the school's new clientele would act and feel entitled. Later that day, I sat at a low, hexagonal table with three kindergarten teachers, eating bag lunches and catching up. I commented on how crowded that morning's tour had been; when families had visited a kindergarten classroom, they had barely managed to squeeze around the margins of the rug area to watch the read-aloud. The teachers were skeptical that any of these school tourists would actually send their children to P.S. 411, since the school had "a lot of Black and Brown kids and kids from the projects." Ms. O'Shea, a White teacher whose classroom was my home base, mocked parents who walked around taking pictures and making "douchey faces" because they could not believe the school was up to their standards. Other teachers shared their frustration and hurt at having their professional skills questioned, telling me stories about parents in the rezoning meetings who had requested that P.S 411 teachers receive additional training to teach academically advanced kids. Ms. O'Shea commented on the irony, reminding her colleagues that private school teachers received much less training than they did. Ms. Smith, a Black teacher, told the lunch table that recently, she saw a tour group that included a White mother from a private day care where Ms. Smith had previously worked. The mother asked her, "Is it *really* okay there?" Ms. Smith sputtered with anger: "First of all, I'm standing near my principal in my classroom. What do you think I'm going to say? Second of all, what do you really think of me? So, you think you can't trust your lovely peach children to me? Are you so concerned that your child's teacher is brown?" These educators were very sure that newcomer parents' perceptions of P.S. 411 were inaccurate. They were also sure that these perceptions were closely tied to race.

It was widely, if implicitly, understood that P.S. 411's largest marketing obstacle was its primarily low-income Black and Latine student body;

its strongest selling point was the school's potential diversity—if only it could be realized. Newcomer families who acted as boosters for the school urged Principal Blake to talk about the school differently, telling her, "You need to clarify that you're about diversity." Ms. Gonzalez, an assistant principal, spoke enthusiastically at the rezoning meeting about how some newcomer families had begun to "bring diversity to the school." It was widely understood that P.S. 411's success depended on the recruitment, enrollment, and retention of gentrifiers—primarily White middle-class or professional families—who were the New York City school system's most special people.

Managing Diversity: "Everyone's Going to Get the Same"

When I asked Principal Blake about the changing student demographics at P.S. 411, she was very clear that her focus was equality: "I've always said that it doesn't matter what race or religion or culture you are. We're going to give kids the same. Everyone's going to get the same." She repeated that sentence for emphasis: "Everyone's going to get the same." Principal Blake's color-evasive approach to diversity was shared by many P.S. 411 teachers. For example, the music teacher Ms. Tanner told me how "amazing" it would be if the school "could be one of those schools that really, like, embraces diversity and makes everyone feel equal." Like Principal Blake, she and her colleagues were committed to a vision of diversity that, ironically, depended on sameness.

Still, P.S. 411 administrators anticipated that some families would ask for special treatment. One afternoon in early May, I sat down with Ms. Diana to discuss how P.S. 411 had changed in the year following the rezoning. She told me, "I see little patterns of things that I think administration needs to be ready for, because I have seen schools that have gentrified." Ms. Diana worried that slowly, families would begin telling teachers and administrators "how to do things." She had already received an email requesting that a child be placed in a particular pre-K class; she also had families asking that their children be placed in classrooms with "their friends from their little preschools." She wondered aloud whether P.S. 411 administrators would soon be hearing from parents about which snacks to serve or how to respond to conflict between two children.

Principal Blake felt strongly that Ms. Diana and other P.S. 411 staff needed to push back against such parental demands. Principal Blake told me that when families made requests related to classroom placement, she always responded by saying, "We have our protocols, and we have a way we do things." She also was quick to point out that it was not just newcomer families who made special requests, reporting that that families living in public housing also made their wishes known—but these were usually "a different kind of demand" that she could more easily address. Still, sticking firmly to her color-evasive stance, Principal Blake laughed and said, "It doesn't matter if you're black, white, purple, or yellow. You're not happy with what the school has decided, you move on."

And yet Principal Blake expected that some families would not, in fact, move on. She implicitly acknowledged this fact as she reflected, "I haven't had the experience *yet* where I've been given an ultimatum of, you know, 'You do this for my child or I'm out.' . . . In terms of, you know, newcomer families, I haven't had that experience yet." That *"yet"* mattered. The fact that Principal Blake expected to receive an ultimatum pointed to both her perceptions of families and the difficulty of sticking to the protocols she had outlined. As the sociologists Amanda Lewis and John Diamond argue, staff in racially and socioeconomically diverse schools are deeply influenced by not only the demands that advantaged families actually advance but also the pushback they anticipate from these families. Furthermore, school staff are not always aware that they take these anticipated demands into account as they make decisions.[46]

Families tended to have other takes on P.S. 411's potential diversity. Nancy, for example, was a White professional woman whose daughter, Hazel, was rezoned to the school a few months before her kindergarten year. Once she got past her initial surprise, Nancy quickly recognized many of P.S. 411's strengths: low student-teacher ratios, a positive school climate, arts and enrichment programming, and well-maintained facilities. Hazel was one of only a handful of White kindergarteners who enrolled at P.S. 411 that year. Nancy appreciated the opportunity for her daughter to be "around different people and, you know, open-minded." What is more, Nancy told me, "I literally don't think there would be any place that was as supportive" as P.S. 411 when Hazel experienced intense separation anxiety at the beginning of kindergarten. Nancy also knew that the school had been given "so many resources and funds." However, P.S. 411 still made Nancy "feel nervous." She asked me apprehensively if Hazel's class was "wild" and whether Hazel would "suffer." It was difficult for Nancy to move past her sense that Hazel might have been better off in a class with "more White kids, just more diversity." She knew P.S. 411 would only realize its potential diversity if a critical mass of families like hers decided to "stick around."

While Nancy saw P.S. 411 as not yet diverse enough, some other parents saw the school as already having reached that goal. Janice, Marquise's mother, was one of what Principal Blake called "our NYCHA [public housing] families." When the time came to enter Marquise in the kindergarten lottery, Janice's primary priorities were convenience (the school was a few blocks away) and "a good atmosphere." Janice told me that she saw the school as benefiting from gentrification, explaining that the new school zone meant that "it has no other choice but to be diverse." Like Nancy, Janice had herself attended racially and ethnically diverse elementary schools. She remembered that experience fondly. She appreciated the opportunity for children to "learn different cultures" and understand that the "world is not just Black and White": "The world is diverse. . . . You got to learn how to deal with different people." On a practical level, Janice also felt sure that "now with the diversity, it also will bring in more funding and more programs." Unlike Nancy, Janice saw her own options as limited, P.S. 411's quality as well established, and the school as already diverse.

The Dilemma of Whiteness in School Diversity

My findings in New York City are far from unique; they reflect patterns very similar to what Cucchiara found in Philadelphia schools and Posey-Maddox observed in the Bay Area.[47] In each of these gentrifying cities, the hidden curriculum of diversity encourages educational policy makers and district administrators to cater to, in Superintendent Arnett's words, "the needs, wants, and desires" of neighborhood newcomers. As Berrey aptly puts it, diversity becomes a "presumptively positive buzzword" that reflects "the interests, worldviews, and experiences of powerful decision makers and their most important constituents—who may include people of color but by and large are White and well off."[48] Staff of the New York City Department of Education, District 41, and P.S. 411 leveraged this buzzword in attempts to bolster student enrollment and redistribute much-needed resources. By doing so, these policy actors opened up and foreclosed various responses to educational injustice, most obviously in their (at times reluctant) decision to center the needs, wants, and desires of the district's "special people."

Policy conversations about school diversity are, in and of themselves, pedagogical: they shape our thinking about what we can and cannot do to address the very real problems facing public schools. Turner argues that appeals to the "instrumental and individualized benefits of racially diverse public schools" may undermine other compelling goals, such as "equity, community, and justice."[49] When district administrators focus on marketing schools to White neighborhood newcomers or when academic researchers describe Black or Latine children in segregated schools as having "low exposure" to White children, they are telling us that schools like P.S. 411 *need* White children and their families. Many twenty-first-century attempts to promote school diversity are therefore rooted in the same assumptions that informed the *Brown* decision: Black and Latine children from low-income families need to sit next to White children from middle-class and professional families in order to receive "a proper education."[50] As neoliberal logics have replaced court mandates with choice policies, responsibility for making schools more diverse has been shifted from policy makers to the administrators who market schools and the families who choose them.

During the District 41 rezoning meeting that I described at the beginning of this chapter, Assistant Principal Gonzalez assured the assembled families and community members that students would thrive in their newly diverse environments: "Our classrooms are our labs, right? That's where children learn to socialize together, to get along together. And so, I say to all of you, learn from the children. See through the eyes of children, because *they* don't see color. They don't see dollar signs. They see friendship. They see friends, and they learn to get along together." Indeed, during the two years I spent observing District 41 and P.S. 411, I repeatedly heard staff dismiss concerns about school demographics as "adult business." Yet it is not possible to separate what children experience inside classrooms from the policies, discourses, and systems in which they are situated. As the education policy scholar Jean Anyon wrote over twenty-five years ago, attempting to fix schools without changing "the city in which they are embedded is like trying to clean the air on one side of a screen door."[51]

In order for P.S. 411 to realize its potential diversity, the school had to recruit and retain neighborhood newcomers; that is one side of the screen door. Yet examining the hidden curriculum of school diversity in adult spaces can only tell us so much. Policies and policy discourses inform what the anthropologist Kysa Nygreen calls "the landscape for interaction" among students, families, and educators, "constraining and enabling particular forms of meaning making" in schools and classrooms.[52] In chapter 2, we will see what happened on the other side of the door, as Nancy's and Janice's children entered their new school and kindergarten classroom.

2

Problem Children and Children with Problems

Learning from Diversity at P.S. 411

In a classroom of eighteen children, Hazel stood out. She was one of two White kids in her class and the only White girl in her grade that year. She was slim and slightly shorter than many of her classmates. She had a blond ponytail with a cowlick that frequently stood up, almost vertically, from the top of her head. Her voice was soft and squeaky.

Hazel loved to make art. Over the course of the school year, she drew flowers and landscapes that decorated the classroom walls, illustrated pictures of her family members to take home, and outlined images of sushi, her favorite food. One day, as she worked on a self-portrait assignment, Hazel made quiet "ooooh" sounds under her breath. First, she carefully wrote "I love mom" on the line at the bottom of the paper where students were asked to describe themselves. Next, she crayoned in an outline of her body that took up the entire page. Hazel chatted happily with her tablemates about her color choices, pausing occasionally to squint and make sure she got the details just right as she filled in her clothes: a yellow polka-dot sweatshirt, leopard-print leggings, and flowers decorating her toes.

Despite Hazel's apparent comfort with many classroom tasks, she and her family had a very difficult start to her kindergarten year. During the second week of school, when she was asked to draw a picture showing her favorite part of the school day, Hazel drew a child and an adult standing in a doorway. When I asked who the people were, she explained, "Me and my mommy." When I asked what part of the school day this was, she replied, "leaving." Hazel's conviction that leaving was the best part of school was not a passing feeling. She cried almost nonstop in class that day—and many days in September—for several hours.

FIGURE 2.1. Hazel, self-portrait, May 2017: "I like running on the treadmill. I always play. I can jump."

Each morning at drop-off, Hazel clung to her mother or father, stalling at the classroom door. About three weeks into the school year, Hazel's hesitation at the entry escalated into full-on rebellion. She screamed and howled and kicked, refusing to go into class. Then she tried to bite her teacher, Ms. O'Shea. After a few minutes of anguished indecision, Hazel's mother, Nancy, took her back home.

When Hazel returned to P.S. 411 the next day, nobody spoke to her about her behavior. However, school staff soon came together to develop a comprehensive plan to support her at drop-off and throughout the day. Looking back at the end of the year, Nancy marveled at everything P.S. 411 had done for Hazel: "I feel like they just forgot about everybody else and zoned in on her. As much as we got, that's what it felt like at least."

Marquise and his family had a very different experience in school. In some ways, Marquise stood out much less at P.S. 411 than Hazel did. Tall

FIGURE 2.2. Marquise, self-portrait, May 2017: "I like to go to school. I am a student. I always be good. I like to eat ice cream."

and stocky, Marquise had dark skin, a round face, and close-cropped hair. He was one of seven Black boys in Ms. O'Shea's class. Like most of his classmates, he and his family lived in public housing down the street from the school.

When Hazel cried throughout the first weeks of September, Marquise sometimes wandered over to her, quietly extending his hand. Hazel held on tight as her tears kept flowing. Marquise often offered hugs to both grown-ups and kids; he was quick to smile and delighted in sharing jokes. One day, he was trailing behind the group as his class walked down the hallway. Ms. O'Shea called down the line, a bit impatiently, asking him to "catch up!" From my station at the end of the line, I heard Marquise tell himself, "Catch up! Catch up!" Then he paused, thinking, and chuckled quietly, "Ketchup! Ketchup! Ketchup!" He shot me a wide grin, shook his head, and hurried after the group.

Despite Marquise's good humor, he often made other students at P.S. 411 nervous because he refused to follow adults' directions. On the first day of school, Marquise moved away from his assigned seat without permission. Ms. O'Shea turned to him and said, "Excuse me!" Several times that day, Ms. O'Shea asked Marquise to "redo" his actions, including sitting quietly and following directions for moving between his table and the rug area. When Ms. O'Shea asked him to practice one more time before dismissal, Marquise rebelled, loudly saying, "No!" Ms. O'Shea immediately pulled him aside, saying, "In this room, we do what grown-ups tell us. If I tell you to do something or Ms. Alex asks you to do something, you say 'Yes, Ms. O'Shea,' and you do it. We need to practice this a lot of times so that you can get it right." Then Ms. O'Shea had Marquise cross the room to the rug again and again, telling him when he had it "almost right" and then praising him highly for doing it perfectly. When Marquise's mother, Janice, came to pick him up at the end of the day, Ms. O'Shea reported what had happened. Janice was quick to tell Marquise that he must always say, "Yes, Ms. O'Shea!" when his teacher asked him a question. After dismissal, Ms. O'Shea told me that Janice had pulled her aside at drop-off that morning to warn that Marquise might have trouble following her directions.

This chapter will examine the different ways that Hazel and Marquise were treated at P.S. 411, inside and outside their classroom. Both kids struggled with the transition to kindergarten, and both repeatedly breached classroom norms throughout the first few weeks of school. However, school staff approached Hazel as a child with a problem who needed support; they treated Marquise as a problem child who needed discipline. Despite a stated commitment to treat all of the students "the same," the staff of P.S. 411 "zoned in" on Hazel as they required Marquise to "practice" his behavior. These different approaches reflected the investment that P.S. 411's leaders had in retaining students like Hazel, whose family was among their school's most "valued customers."[1]

The leaders of P.S. 411, like many diversity advocates, believed that students like Marquise would benefit from the resources that students like Hazel could bring to their school. But in this case, those benefits did not appear. The special care that the school exhibited for Hazel's well-being included dedicated time, attention, and support that were not offered to Marquise. What is more, the school's differentiated treatment and resource allocation profoundly shaped the racialized lessons that Hazel, Marquise, and their classmates learned at their diverse school.

The Staff and Students of P.S. 411

The staff of P.S. 411 believed in their school. Many teachers and administrators, about 50 percent of whom were Black and 50 percent of whom were White, had actively chosen to work in a school that served almost exclusively low-income Black and Latine children. Every long-term staff member I interviewed shared vivid stories about how hard they had worked over the years to become, in the words of school security guard Ms. Knox, "a community where everybody looks out for everybody, and we help each other." Mr. Williams, a Black man who had served as the school's parent coordinator for fifteen years, believed that what made

P.S. 411 "great" was its genuine care for children and families. Like Ms. Blake, the school's principal, Mr. Williams believed that the school best demonstrated this care by treating people "the same":

> If you come in here, and you're teaching children at *this* level [gesturing toward the floor], because you believe that on the color their skin, they're not going to understand up *here* [pointing at the ceiling], but then you see somebody else come in, a different economic status, a different nationality, and you believe they're *here* [pointing high again], so you're going to start teaching *there*—no. You shouldn't be a teacher. . . . Everybody should be treated the same. And when we're teaching at a low level or if we're treating children differently because of economics or nationality, then we're wrong. We're wrong. And we're supposed to be building future leaders. If we're not doing that, then we're wrong.

Mr. Williams believed his school was responsible for holding students to high standards; those standards would not and should not change "according to who came in here."

All the same, P.S. 411 staff paid careful attention to who enrolled in the school. In a lunchtime conversation I had with two kindergarten teachers, they told me that in the past, there had been, at most, "a sprinkle" of White children in their classrooms. They explained that in previous years, that sprinkle of White students had transferred to other schools after pre-K or kindergarten, although a few "might try" first grade. Ms. Diana, a White woman who was the assistant principal in charge of the school's primary grades, told me she noticed "right off the bat" how the changes to P.S. 411 zone lines had shifted student demographics. When I asked her to describe the impact of the rezoning, she explained that for the four years she had worked at the school, there had been "definitely a population of children here that are extremely needy, whether it's emotionally, financially. They've been through experiences that young children shouldn't have to go through. They've been traumatized. They've been removed from their parents through ACS cases. Their caregiver is maybe a drug addict, maybe incarcerated, so that's an ongoing concern." Ms. Diana told me with a sigh that the school tries to "help take care of the community," but "you can only do so much." She explained that if kids "acted out" or were "aggressive" due to their trauma, it could be difficult for them to "blend" with neighborhood newcomers in order to "coexist as a community." She worried that the new "demographic of families that are affluent" might therefore decide that P.S. 411 "might not be the right place for them." As we saw in chapter 1, P.S. 411 staff had worked hard to counter public perceptions of their segregated school, allocating significant resources (including their own time and effort) in hopes of attracting and retaining neighborhood newcomers. They could not allow student behavior to impede the school's potential diversity.

Ms. Diana's concerns reflected common perceptions of Black, Latine, and low-income students. Her descriptions of students as "needy," "traumatized," or "aggressive" illustrate ways that urban students and their families are often perceived. This deficit framing also informs how schools respond to student behavior. Student demographics—and the significance we attribute to them—have real consequences for how educators perceive and respond to children.[2] Schools and districts with large populations of Black students are more likely to implement policies and practices that criminalize children, while districts with primarily White students are more likely to medicalize children and provide them with behavioral support plans.[3] In other words, schools that serve primarily Black students are likely to treat them as problem kids; schools that serve primarily White students are likely to treat them as kids with problems.

P.S. 411 staff were particularly concerned about the experiences of newcomer families enrolled in the entry grades of kindergarten and pre-kindergarten. I was interested in how staff perceived students who were brand new to the school and therefore had not yet developed a reputation among the teachers. I therefore decided to spend most of my time at the school in Ms. O'Shea's kindergarten classroom, K-301. Like other early childhood classrooms, K-301 was more likely to include children whose families were gentrifiers. The year I observed, there were eighteen children in K-301. Thirteen of these students lived in public housing, four lived in apartments within a few blocks of the school, and one commuted each day from a homeless shelter in another borough. Fifteen students were Black, and one was Latine. The other two students in the class were Hazel and Felix: both White, both the children of professionals, both living in recently built condominiums, and both assigned to P.S. 411 due to the recent changes to the school's catchment zone.

Becoming a Good Student: How Race and Gender Influence Reputation

Hazel's behavior at the beginning of the school year puzzled Ms. O'Shea and many P.S. 411 staff. Her outbursts did not fit their belief that Hazel was a "good" student. "Good" students, as many of us are well aware, are compliant. They follow the classroom rules, sitting still and following directions, earning gold stars, and accepting the adult authority that undergirds the hidden curriculum of schooling. They successfully negotiate conflicting expectations of competition and sharing, participation and quietness, and independence and compliance that are common in early childhood classrooms.[4] What is more, they are seen to be doing so. They may not always listen perfectly, but they are recognized as good listeners.

Children's reputations play a central role in how adults respond to them. In the words of the early childhood scholar Maggie MacLure and her colleagues, "reputation is a public matter." After "a child becomes a problem in the eyes of others," their reputation hardens relatively rapidly and then becomes deeply entrenched over the course of an academic year.[5] Teachers and classmates alike are quick to apply raced and gendered labels such as "smart," "troublemaker," or "tomboy" to kids, labels that influence their interpretations of how children interact with their peers, with adults, and with the curriculum.[6] After the child's reputation has hardened, their behavior is read through and reinscribes those lenses.[7] School staff respond accordingly.

Many educators are aware that reputation has important consequences for how a child is perceived by educators, classmates, and even teachers who have not ever met the kid in question. However, both teachers and researchers may pay less attention to the ways that students' reputations are tied to their race and gender.[8] Race, gender, and age are, in the sociologist Cecilia Ridgeway's terms, "primary categories" that influence our interpretations of human behavior due to "common, cultural knowledge" underlying our social interactions.[9] What is more, our constructions of feminine and masculine roles are themselves racialized.[10] By age five, Black girls are often seen as less innocent and more disruptive than their White peers are.[11] As the teacher educator Joseph Nelson argues, many educators are unable to approach Black boys "as children whose actions communicate both met and unmet needs."[12] Black boys and girls are both significantly more likely than White children to be viewed as adults, criminals, or other than human.[13]

These raced and gendered childhoods have troubling implications for how educators perceive and respond to even very young students.[14] Early childhood educators anticipate and look out for more challenging behavior from Black children.[15] They are also more likely to focus on enforcing rules and delivering consequences, rather than facilitating relationships or rewarding positive behavior, with boys than with girls.[16] This may be related to the fact that elementary classrooms are highly likely to be taught by White women, who may identify with and presume the innocence of children who resemble themselves.[17] However, racial inequalities in school discipline extend far beyond how individual teachers respond to individual students. As John Diamond and Louis Gomez write, "school discipline policies are written about and understood in race-neutral terms," but at each step of the disciplinary routine, "white supremacy and anti-Black racism lead Black students to suffer worse experiences and outcomes."[18] Diamond and Lewis argue that this is in large part because Black students (and, I would add, boys) are treated as "inherently suspect," while White students (and, I would add, girls) are treated as "inherently innocent."[19] I was therefore not surprised to observe many P.S. 411 staff quickly labeling Marquise as misbehaving; their presumptions fit widespread narratives about troubled Black boys.[20] Throughout the year, however, I often wondered exactly when and how staff decided that Hazel was "good."

Hazel's Reputation: Standing Out at P.S. 411

Hazel, unlike many of her peers at P.S. 411, lived in a luxury apartment building completed only two years earlier; her parents, an adjunct art professor and a freelance writer, qualified for reduced rent in the development under New York City's affordable housing policy. Hazel's parents and P.S. 411 staff periodically commented on the literal and figurative distances between their apartment building, eight blocks away, and the homes of her classmates who lived in public housing down the street.

The week before school began, I spent an afternoon helping Ms. O'Shea organize her classroom. Ms. O'Shea was a White woman who had taught at P.S. 411 for over ten years, always in the early grades. She had a reputation as one of the school's strongest teachers; her expertise in instruction and classroom management was frequently cited by her colleagues, school administrators, and families. As we wiped down classroom tables, set up the dramatic play area, and created a word wall, Ms. O'Shea told me that the previous year was the first time she had kindergarteners who lived in "these fancy buildings around here. Kids were just coming with a lot of experience . . . They traveled; they had been places. They had a larger vocabulary. They had different experiences. They would inspire the other kids." I listened, noting Ms. O'Shea's assumption that kids who lived in "fancy buildings" served as role models and resources for other students. Whereas Mr. Williams had described the importance of preparing *all* P.S. 411 students to be "future leaders," Ms. O'Shea seemed to view neighborhood newcomers as uniquely prepared to be leaders in her classroom.

Ms. O'Shea was not the only teacher who saw the new P.S. 411 students as special. The whole school seemed to notice ways in which Hazel and Felix, the other White student in K-301, stood out. When I asked the art teacher about the students of K-301, she told me that Hazel and Felix seemed "really smart"; unlike many of their classmates, they were able to "pay attention" and stay focused on learning. One rainy day, the younger grades streamed into the school auditorium to watch a video montage created for prospective P.S. 411 parents. When they saw Hazel and Felix featured, their classmates called out their names and cheered from the audience. While nobody ever explicitly commented on their whiteness, both adults and children regularly pointed out the many ways that Hazel and Felix were exceptional.

This exemplary status became particularly clear in the moments when Ms. O'Shea positioned Hazel and Felix as role models for the rest of the class. When a new kid was talking loudly and making silly faces at his table, Ms. O'Shea turned to Felix and said, "*You* know what to do. You help him with his behavior by being the leader that you are." Ms. O'Shea frequently pointed out when Hazel did "the right thing": "Interesting questions, Hazel! Hazel's noticing a lot of details. That's what happens when your brain focuses on the right thing, when it focuses on school." Felix and Hazel were not the only students Ms. O'Shea praised in public. However, the frequency with which she did so was notable.

The pattern was clear not only to me, as an observer, but also to Hazel and Felix's classmates. One day, for example, Ms. Diana stopped by the class and asked Ms. O'Shea to choose a student to run an errand to the front office. Ms. O'Shea looked up and down the line of kindergartners waiting by the door, lined up for gym. She selected Hazel because "she's the only one standing still and quiet in her line spot." Then she allowed Hazel to choose a classmate to go with her. The remaining students quickly stood up straight. After some deliberation, Hazel chose Felix to be her partner. Ms. O'Shea and Ms. Diana immediately remarked on what a good choice Hazel had made. The other children groaned their disappointment, but nobody appeared surprised.

Ms. O'Shea was very committed to maintaining a calm, orderly classroom. She immediately corrected any "bad choices" the students made, requiring them to practice following instructions and making it clear when they failed to meet her expectations. For example, she told one girl who ignored directions while giggling on the rug, "I'm very sad. My heart is breaking. You know better, you know how to behave. I know you do because I know your mommy, and I know she taught you better." Ms. O'Shea frequently leveraged praise for kids' "good choices"—as when she enthusiastically told students, "Kiss your brain," if they got an answer right—to serve a parallel purpose. One day, she told the class, "I'm going to give Hazel the first chance because Hazel was sitting there like such a big girl, like a first grader, the whole time we were on the rug." Ms. O'Shea then reminded students, "If you are on your best behavior, then I will notice it."

In fact, Ms. O'Shea had identified Hazel as a positive role model from the outset. On the very first day of school, Ms. O'Shea told the class that Hazel was "really good" because she had figured out where to put her things away without asking. She explicitly praised Hazel's classroom behavior almost every time I observed: "Thank you, Hazel! . . . I see Hazel's ready and waiting!" By doing so, she called attention to Hazel's outstanding qualities, making comments such as "Hazel went right to her spot, sat crisscross applesauce, and kept her voice off. She was the only one!" This public praise of Hazel's exceptional behavior was a powerful reminder that "goodness" is generally marked by compliance—a defining characteristic of white femininity.[21] As the only White kindergarten girl in her gentrifying school, Hazel was already likely to draw attention; in the words of her mother, Nancy, she was "easy to pick out in the bunch." Her emerging reputation for docility made her stand out even more.

Hazel stood out for not only what she did but also what she did not do. In addition to praising Hazel as "always ready," Ms. O'Shea told the class several times that Hazel's "brain focuses on the right thing." Indeed, one day when the students were sitting on the rug, a classmate pouted and dramatically sighed, "Ohhhhh," after Ms. O'Shea chose Hazel to read out loud. Ms. O'Shea was quick to reprimand the kid, asking pointedly, "Does Hazel ever do that when you're called on?" The child silently shook her head no. Hazel had the reputation of an ideal kindergarten student.

Hazel's Diagnosis: "Anxiety Is a Terrible Emotion"

Despite Hazel's reputation for goodness, both adults and children worried about her. For the first three months of the school year, Hazel could not make it through the entire school day without breaking down into expansive, extended tears. Her teachers and classmates were quite concerned about Hazel's palpable discomfort; school staff discussed her behavior in murmured tones, and kids offered hugs when Hazel quietly sobbed. After several days when Hazel would not enter her classroom, Ms. Diana began taking Hazel to her office at the start of each school day, where they played games together until Ms. Diana slowly coaxed Hazel to go to class. However, the need for this intervention did not fit with Hazel's reputation for compliance, and so Ms. Diana and Ms. O'Shea encouraged her family to request the support of a child psychologist. Hazel's parents quickly agreed.

Dr. Medina was on site several days each week as part of a community partnership intended to support low-income children at P.S. 411, but she was available to treat any prekindergartener, kindergartener, or first grader who was referred to her. She told me that in the seven years she had worked at P.S. 411, almost all of her referrals had come from teachers or the principal. In the year following the rezoning, however, Dr. Medina's referral list looked "totally different": she had "more White kids, more middle-class and professional parents" who had self-referred, which had never happened before. If she had space in her schedule, Dr. Medina accepted these self-referrals. Once spots on Dr. Medina's schedule were occupied, there was limited room for her to add other children to her caseload. As a result, families who self-referred early (like Hazel's) were more likely to receive her support. This year, Dr. Medina's caseload included a substantial number of self-referrals from White families.

After Dr. Medina had spoken with Hazel's parents, observed Ms. O'Shea's class, and met with Hazel several times, she diagnosed Hazel with anxiety. Following this diagnosis, Dr. Medina counseled both Hazel and her parents (separately and together) for several months. She also occasionally came to K-301 to offer Ms. O'Shea strategies to support Hazel in the classroom. Soon, Ms. O'Shea relied on the anxiety diagnosis to make sense of Hazel's behavior. As a matter of principle, Ms. O'Shea expected children to take responsibility for their actions. She spoke to the class frequently about the importance of making good choices, and she was quick to deliver immediate consequences for unauthorized actions. When she discussed Hazel's classmates, Ms. O'Shea often described their "misbehavior" with frustration, adding her thoughts about their parents' mistakes. However, this did not happen with Hazel.

One day after school in October, Ms. O'Shea caught me up on some events I had missed the week before. She said that Hazel had a series of "wild and wicked temper tantrums." She had even screamed, "I hate Ms. O'Shea! I hate Ms. O'Shea! I don't want to stay with her! I hate school!" Then, Hazel tried to bite her teacher. After Ms. O'Shea told me this story, she shrugged. She said that it was okay for Hazel not to like her. She knew that "anxiety is a terrible emotion"; then she paused, correcting herself, and said, "state of mind." It appeared that Hazel's diagnosis relieved her of responsibility for her behavior in Ms. O'Shea's eyes; the diagnosis shaped not only how she responded to Hazel's behavior but also who she understood Hazel to be. This made it possible for Hazel to preserve her reputation as innocent, despite behavior that might have tarnished the reputations of her peers.

The diagnostic frame also shaped the institutional support that P.S. 411 offered Hazel. After the morning when Hazel attacked Ms. O'Shea, Ms. Diana sat down with Hazel's parents and her teacher. Together, they decided that until Hazel's anxiety about school had subsided, she would leave kindergarten after lunchtime each day. When I asked Ms. Diana later how they had reached this decision, she told me, "We needed to support Hazel. We needed to support the family. We needed to work out a plan." I wondered aloud how it was possible to just decide that Hazel could leave school midway through each day. Was it not against the rules? Ms. Diana told me that when she shared her plan with other staff members, "I didn't have anybody telling me no because the focus is what's right for this child." Then she paused and noted that somebody from the Department of Education *had* explicitly told her several weeks before, "You cannot have a pre-K child come for half a day without permission from the DOE." However, Ms. Diana said with a wink and a smile, nothing had been said about *kindergarteners*—and she had never asked.

Rather than criminalizing Hazel's behavior, P.S. 411 took an approach that affirmed her innocence. She received an individualized program of half-day kindergarten until the week after Thanksgiving, when—to her parents' and teachers' delight—she suddenly stopped asking to go home early. For ten weeks, Hazel's classmates accepted without question that Hazel left school before lunch. They did not comment when she left the room to talk with Dr. Medina. In fact, perhaps because she was only available at certain times, playtime with Hazel seemed to become even more desirable. When she returned to class, her friends frequently rushed over to give her hugs, at times overwhelming her. Ms. O'Shea was quick to protect Hazel, telling the class that they needed to give her a little more space.

Hazel's diagnosis, together with her reputation as an ideal student, did more than facilitate a view of Hazel's behavior as beyond her control. Her exceptional status also allowed staff to relax rules that might otherwise have been quite rigid. P.S. 411 extended resources to and developed accommodations for Hazel. By working flexibly to support and retain these exceptional newcomers, the school treated both Hazel and her family as special people.

Hazel's Family: "A Very Secure Home Life"

P.S. 411 staff's perceptions of Hazel appeared tightly tied to their perceptions of her family. In separate conversations with me, Principal Blake, Ms. Diana, and Ms. O'Shea all distinguished Hazel from her peers who lived "down the street" in public housing. Ms. Diana explained that "a child like Hazel obviously is—experiences things with her parents. Her parents talk to her. She has a very secure home life." She explicitly compared Hazel's home with the homes of "a lot of our kids" whose "parents talk *at* them rather than *to* them." I probed further:

> ALEX: So, you weren't worried or aren't worried about Hazel in the way that you'd be worried about the other kids?
>
> Ms. DIANA: No. No, I didn't see anything else. I really saw that she was just struggling with anxiety. I didn't feel that she was not being taken care of. We have kids who come in here who just reek. They haven't been bathed. They come in for breakfast. They're ravenous. Some kids who would just eat all day if we let them.
>
> ALEX: It's a different situation?
>
> Ms. DIANA: Yeah, and again, that's socioeconomic. [pause] I don't know if that's exactly the right way to say it or—for Hazel, it was just that really severe anxiety.

Ms. Diana's comments reminded me of Ellen Berrey's argument that many decision-makers use diversity "to draw contrasts" and "to vilify aspects of social life as threatened, denigrated, or inferior."[22] Because the student body at P.S. 411 was gentrifying, staff had abundant opportunities to compare their perceptions of the home lives and communities of gentrifiers and longtime residents. Hazel's presence within the school appeared to foreground the dysfunction that educators perceived among her classmates' families. Ms. Diana was quite confident that Hazel's parents, unlike other P.S. 411 families, could not be held responsible for Hazel's problems. What is more, she perceived Hazel's behavior as an individual problem, rather than a symptom of community pathology. Hazel's reputation was thus intricately linked to that of her family and, more broadly, her race, socioeconomic status, and status as a neighborhood newcomer.

Like Ms. Diana, Ms. O'Shea was quick to describe Hazel's mother and father as "good parents" who were "firm" and "caring, kind people." However, she added, she had seen them inadvertently encourage Hazel's behavior at times. Other members of P.S. 411 were a bit more willing to locate responsibility for Hazel's behavior in her family. Ms. Knox, the school security guard, was sure that Hazel's parents were quite anxious themselves. A Black woman who had worked at P.S. 411 for over a decade, Ms. Knox was a beloved member of the school community. She welcomed kids and families warmly each morning and watched over students as they passed by her hallway station throughout the day. When I asked Ms. Knox what she had noticed about Hazel during drop-off, she first detailed Hazel's many attempts to run away. Then she explained,

> I told her mother, I said, "You gotta leave her. You gotta leave her because she has to know that you mean business and that it hurts you, because [of] this anxiety and separation. However, you have to let her know that it's okay. . . . Because she has to learn how to be alone and okay at the same time." . . . When Dad brought her, Dad would, like, fall to pieces. I said, "Dad, she'll be okay. If you want to, you can leave the classroom, but you don't have to leave the building. And just walk back in and check and see, check on her." And he did, and he was like, "Well, she's okay." I said, "She'll be okay."

Ms. Knox and Ms. O'Shea implied that Hazel's separation anxiety was not an anomaly; rather, it was rooted in ongoing family dynamics. At times, their comments echoed popular tropes about "helicopter parents," with attendant race- and class-based stereotypes. However, they also approved of the ways that Hazel's family advocated for her, without appearing to recognize that this advocacy was closely tied to their racial and economic status. Ultimately, P.S. 411 staff were reluctant to find anyone in the family responsible for Hazel's challenges.

It is worth noting that when Hazel took a break from class by going to Ms. Diana's office or therapy with Dr. Medina, she went to some of the only support spaces at P.S. 411 that were under the care of White women. This was far from inevitable: five of the six administrators at the school were Black or Latine. However, Ms. Diana (a White woman) was the assistant principal in charge of kindergarten, and it was she who encouraged Hazel's family to ask Dr. Medina (another White woman) for help. It so happened that Hazel was placed in Ms. O'Shea's classroom (also a White woman), rather than that of any of the three other kindergarten teachers, who were all women of color. The school's willingness to provide Hazel with flexible support may in part have been because these White women seemed to see Hazel and her family as people very much like themselves. Early in the year, Ms. Diana told me that her own son had "pretty tough separation anxiety," and that is how she knew both how to help Hazel and how challenging anxiety might be for her family. Ms. O'Shea nurtured a relationship with Hazel based on shared experiences. When Hazel brought in a cream cheese and jelly sandwich for lunch, for example, Ms. O'Shea smiled and said that her own mother used to make that sandwich for her when she was little. This interaction contrasted sharply with Ms. O'Shea's running commentary about food that Hazel's classmates brought from home, which she deemed unhealthy—a label often assigned to the parenting practices of women of color.[23] Ms. Diana and Ms. O'Shea were quick to note deficits in Hazel's classmates, their families, and the subsidized housing residents that the school had long served, as White educators often do with low-income students and families of color.[24] They did not do so with Hazel, her parents, or many families who were new to P.S. 411.

Hazel's mother, Nancy, felt confident that the school was taking good care of her daughter. She marveled at the "time and energy" that P.S. 411

staff spent on Hazel, telling me that the way they treated her "as a little individual" was "extraordinary." Nancy did not pause to ask why Hazel's continued presence at P.S. 411 may have felt so important to school staff, who told me privately that they were not sure Hazel would stay on for first grade. They were right to wonder. During our interview at the end of the year, Nancy asked for my expert opinion: Should Hazel remain at P.S. 411? She liked that Hazel was learning to be comfortable in many settings, and she was so impressed by how the school had "zoned in" with support. But she also worried that Hazel's differences from her classmates exacerbated her anxiety. Nancy could not let go of her fear that P.S. 411 did not have *enough* "diversity."

Marquise's Reputation: A Problem Child with a Problem Family

P.S. 411 dedicated many resources—Ms. Diana's time, Dr. Medina's counseling, and Ms. O'Shea's attention—to easing Hazel's transition to kindergarten. In contrast, Marquise and his mother, Janice, were treated very differently.

Like Hazel, Marquise repeatedly breached classroom norms in big and small ways over the first few weeks of school. Unlike Hazel, Marquise expressed his resistance with defiance, rather than tears. He refused to sit in his assigned rug spot; he shouted out protests during class discussions; he yelled when he did not get selected for the activity center of his choice. In response, Ms. O'Shea tried to gain Marquise's compliance through a range of strategies: she volubly praised him or gave him stickers as rewards for following directions; she called Janice on speaker phone to describe his misbehavior; she kept him in from recess. Nothing seemed to work. At times, Marquise lay down on the floor, wailing loudly and violently kicking his legs, interrupting all other classroom activity. In one such moment, he knocked over a chair. In the first few months of school, Ms. O'Shea often called Mr. Williams or Ms. Knox to get help with Marquise's disruptions. One of them would come to class and take Marquise elsewhere to calm down almost every week.

Marquise rapidly acquired a reputation as a problem child. At times, Ms. O'Shea's low expectations for Marquise became almost explicit. For example, one day when both Marquise and Felix were chatting instead of waiting quietly to be called to the lunch line, Ms. O'Shea looked at Marquise and said, "You're not ready to line up." She turned to Felix next, saying, "Felix, you're not ready. I expect better from you." A week later, Marquise and Xavier, another classmate, were tussling on the rug while Ms. O'Shea was across the room. Ms. O'Shea looked at the two boys and called out, "Stop! Stop!" She went to Marquise, saying, "You're getting out of control," and encouraged him to "take a breath and calm down." She did not say a word to Xavier, who had been lying on top of Marquise. Marquise's peers picked up on Ms. O'Shea's implicit messages. The next week, a child sat in the corner of the classroom passing judgment on his classmates: "Brianna is good! Felix is good! Marquise is bad!"

Ms. O'Shea was doing her best, but she was very frustrated. By the third week of school, she had altered classroom rules for Marquise, allowing him to eat a snack in the midmorning, even though the rest of the class had to wait to eat until lunchtime. It did not seem to help. Neither did anything else. Ms. O'Shea had been teaching young children for more than a decade, and she had developed many classroom management strategies; she did not know why none of them were effective. She looked for another explanation for Marquise's behavior. In search of a diagnosis, she told me that Marquise must have "special needs, ADHD [attention deficit hyperactivity disorder], I don't know," exclaiming with rising exasperation that Marquise should not be in her classroom because he needed a "special setting." Ms. O'Shea asked Ms. Orozco, the school's special education coordinator, to observe Marquise in class and confirm her suspicions. After an hour of observation, Ms. Orozco told Ms. O'Shea that Marquise showed no signs of a disability. Rather, she concluded that Marquise's behavioral choices were a consequence of "learned behavior."

When I talked with Marquise's mother at the end of the school year, Janice told me that this was not the first time that Marquise had "behavior problems" at school. It had happened in preschool too. Janice had previously worked as a substitute teacher, and she knew that Marquise's behavior was unacceptable: "As a teacher, you empathize. You understand that a classroom full of kids—you know it's not just one child that's with the outbursts and the tantrums." She made her expectations very explicit to Marquise: "When you're in school, Ms. O'Shea is your mother. And everybody else is the family. They're going to assist. She can't stop to just focus on you. She has other kids that she needs to focus on." Janice did not want P.S. 411 staff to "zone in" on Marquise, as Hazel's mother had. She wanted Marquise to learn how to stop standing out.

Still, Marquise continued to protest when he was told what to do. After many calls home, Ms. O'Shea invited Janice to a meeting with her and Ms. Orozco to strategize. Janice looked forward to the meeting: she was grateful for the opportunity to get "a full grasp" of what was going on with Marquise so she could figure out what her child needed. She told me later that during their conversation, she was very direct with Ms. O'Shea and Ms. Orozco, saying, "Look, he needs help. . . . I need help. I don't know what to do. I don't even know what to do." Janice saw herself as Ms. O'Shea's ally; she was open to any ideas about what she could do at home to reinforce the messages his teachers were delivering at school.

Ms. O'Shea and Ms. Orozco saw the situation differently. Following their meeting with Janice, Ms. Orozco warned Ms. O'Shea that the behavior plan they had developed for Marquise would take a long time to work because "mom is not going to keep her end of the bargain." She blamed Marquise's family for his behavior, saying that "he's never had consequences" at home and wondering whether Janice felt guilty about holding Marquise "accountable" since his "dad is not in the picture." Ms. Orozco's comment drew on inaccurate stereotypes about single mothers. It also ignored the artwork displayed behind her on the classroom wall that Marquise and his mother had made together for a "My Family" assignment. The poster included a photograph labeled, "This is me and my dad," in which Marquise and his father proudly smiled and hugged at a preschool graduation ceremony. Although P.S. 411 staff were reluctant to assign blame to Hazel's family for her behavior, they were quick to do so in Marquise's case.

On the basis of very little information, both Marquise and his family had established a reputation—a reputation that overlapped considerably with common perceptions of low-income children and families of color. This was part of a broader pattern. P.S. 411 staff frequently used deficit frames to describe their students who lived in public housing; during lunch breaks, I regularly heard kindergarten teachers describe their students as "extreme" and attribute what I considered typical five-year-old behavior (such as children teasing each other) to shortcomings rooted in "their environment." In Marquise's case, school staff did not seem to recognize Janice's attempts to advocate for and support her son. Janice told me that she simply could not drop everything and go to school if Marquise needed attention: "I can't always get here. I can't always do certain things." Neither did her work schedule allow Janice to volunteer in the classroom, as Hazel's mother, Nancy, did. But she talked frequently with Ms. O'Shea; she came to school for her meeting with Ms. O'Shea and Ms. Orozco; and, a few weeks later, she asked Ms. O'Shea to initiate a special education evaluation. When Ms. O'Shea passed this request on to Ms. Orozco, Ms. Orozco replied that Marquise would not qualify for services since his behavior did not affect his academic performance. He was not evaluated.

Near the end of the school year, I asked Ms. O'Shea if she or Ms. Orozco had ever considered referring Marquise to Dr. Medina for psychological support. They had not. Occasionally when Dr. Medina was in the classroom observing Hazel, I saw her speak quietly to Marquise when he got upset, but that was the extent of her involvement. This surprised me, given how rapidly staff had encouraged Hazel's family to reach out for professional counseling. Dr. Medina had been placed in a gentrifying school through a community partnership intended to support children who lived in public housing. Marquise was one such child. But Dr. Medina treated Hazel, not Marquise. Not only did P.S. 411 staff see the two children differently; they also allocated resources differently.

One day in early November, Ms. O'Shea exclaimed to me that Marquise had tried to "beat [her] up." She reported that when I had been observing another school the previous day, Marquise had attempted (but failed) to kick, hit, and bite her. Soon after, Principal Blake informally assigned a paraprofessional to work with Marquise. She warned, however, that she did not have the funding needed to sustain this intervention, since Marquise did not receive special education services. As he received one-on-one attention, Marquise's behavior changed—slowly, incrementally, and not at all linearly. A few weeks later, however, his paraprofessional was reassigned. The next week, Marquise hit another student on the rug. Ms. O'Shea was fed up. She filed an incident report, and Marquise received an in-school suspension. For two days, he sat in the parent coordinator's office with Mr. Williams.

School staff and Marquise's mother considered that disciplinary event a turning point, telling me that Marquise was "a changed boy" when he returned to K-301. At the end of the year, Ms. O'Shea told me that after his suspension, Marquise rethought his behavior: "You could see him, when he was gearing up to make a choice, kind of slow down and remember how uncomfortable it was to not be with his class, and he would pivot. I think that was the tipping point. I think he got a lot of support, and that helped; but he ultimately needed to hit a brick wall." Ms. O'Shea attributed the change in Marquise to his new understanding that there were consequences for his actions. She saw Marquise as making bad choices, and so she held him responsible for his behavior in a way that she did not hold Hazel responsible for hers.

Mr. Williams agreed that Marquise needed to feel consequences for his behavior, but he attributed the intervention's success to another factor: love. According to Mr. Williams, Marquise needed to hear someone say,

> "Hey, I'm concerned about you. When I tell you 'I love you,' I really love you. This is not—I'm not telling you this so I can get you to do some work. No. On top of my six children at home, I have 398 other children in

here." And they all [the students] know this. "My love for you runs deep like that. I want to see you excel, and I'm going to do everything I possibly can to help that." . . . Now Marquise loves me. He trusts me. He knows, "If I do good, Mr. Williams is going to be right there with me, and if I do bad, he's going to get on me. *But* he's not going to leave me. He's still going to have my back." And that's all children want to know.

Rather than the "brick wall" of a disciplinary consequence, Mr. Williams believed that it was his relationship with Marquise that changed his behavior. Janice agreed. She told me that while some parents might be very upset if their kid got suspended, "I'm not that parent." She knew Marquise's behavior was "not acceptable at all," and she was sure Mr. Williams had helped her son understand that. Most importantly, she explained that "Mr. Williams still didn't make him feel bad about" sitting in his office. According to Janice, Mr. Williams gave Marquise the message, "You may hate being in here, but you're gonna be my friend. We gonna be cool. We gonna do this." That was the message that Marquise needed to hear. Mr. Williams believed it was his responsibility as an educator to have every child's back, regardless of their reputation.

However, Marquise's reputation for "being bad" had already hardened among many other school staff. All the adults who had contact with kindergarteners kept a very close eye on Marquise's behavior. When I stopped at the school entrance one afternoon to ask Ms. Knox how she was doing, the first thing she told me was that the day had gone smoothly because Marquise had stayed calm. In June, I asked Principal Blake and several other staff what they thought about Hazel's and Marquise's progress over the course of the year. An assistant principal told me, "Hazel had difficulty, you know, detaching from her family. Marquise coming in was maybe a little erratic." Principal Blake agreed. She made an offhand reference to the time that Marquise kicked Ms. O'Shea. I paused and told her that it was Hazel who had actually kicked Ms. O'Shea, although Marquise had also tried. Principal Blake was very surprised: "Oh, *she* kicked Ms. O'Shea? Oh, I thought Marquise was the one who kicked Ms. O'Shea. . . . Isn't that interesting!" Principal Blake was so sure that Marquise had been the culprit. It was hard for her to reconcile Hazel's actions with her reputation.

What K-301 Learned from Diversity

Sitting on the classroom rug or perched with kids at their kindergarten tables, I frequently asked myself what their classmates learned from watching Hazel and Marquise. Despite the school's emphasis on treating everyone "the same," K-301 reflected the many ways in which Hazel and Marquise were treated differently. Everybody was clear on what mattered to Ms. O'Shea, and many kids shared her opinions. When I asked six kids to name their three closest friends in the class, five out of six named Hazel. They knew that Ms. O'Shea recognized Hazel as a classroom leader. Aida, a Black girl who was Hazel's closest friend, told me that Ms. O'Shea said that she and Hazel are "the only ones who are kinda doing good" and "sometimes Felix too." Aida and the other students of K-301 were paying attention.

Marquise, like his classmates, knew that it was important to follow instructions. When we spoke in March, he told me that earlier in the year, Ms. O'Shea sometimes had to "talk to [him]," and when that happened, he would end up without "a choice to make." But now, Marquise proudly told me, "I always be good." When a new student joined the class in February and did not follow Ms. O'Shea's instructions, Marquise and his classmates were shocked. Marquise told the kids at his table that when *he* had acted badly, he had experienced the consequences: "I got sent to Mr. Williams three times in one day." Then he turned to Ms. O'Shea, asking how old the other student was. Ms. O'Shea said he was five, and Marquise was shocked: "What, a five-year-old who doesn't know how to act? *I* know how to act right!" In spite of his reputation, Marquise was sure he had learned to make good choices.

However, other kids were not as confident of Marquise's goodness. That spring, I asked kindergarteners to name someone who behaved badly in class. Four out of five named Marquise, citing his lack of compliance with rules, his tendency to hit when frustrated, and his bad listening. One girl told me that she loved Ms. O'Shea because "when Marquise is hitting or fighting or hitting a person, Miss O'Shea protects us."

Over the course of their kindergarten year, Hazel and Marquise's classmates learned that Hazel (White and female) was good but Marquise (Black and male) was not. They learned that they needed protection from children like Marquise. They learned to be patient and flexible with children like Hazel, who required and deserved their protection. They learned that students were responsible for making good choices and that Marquise repeatedly failed to do so. They learned that their school would offer flexible support to some, but not all, children who broke the rules.

Every classroom has students who are known to be good and bad. Ms. O'Shea's was no different. However, the understandings that K-301 students developed aligned neatly with common assumptions that low-income children of color are the primary beneficiaries of school diversity. Of course, these similarities are not a coincidence. Adult decisions about how kids should behave and what they should learn is, as the educator Carla Shalaby writes, "active political work, cultural work."[25] Teachers may consider the organization of their classrooms and their curricula to be racially neutral, but the trends at P.S. 411 were clear.[26] Principal Blake, Mr. Williams, and Ms. O'Shea may have tried to ensure that everyone "gets the same," but they failed to reach that goal.

The Costs and Benefits of Diversity

Both Hazel and Marquise breached school norms during their transition into kindergarten, disrupting instructional activities and at times acting aggressively toward their teacher. But while Hazel developed a reputation for "anxiety" and her family was seen as "caring, kind people,"

Marquise and his mother were held responsible for his "learned behavior." The same assumptions that assigned Marquise and his family responsibility for his actions sheltered Hazel's family from responsibility for hers. Nobody felt the need to teach Hazel a lesson. Hazel's special status offered her protection, while Marquise was subjected to suspicion and surveillance and was repeatedly told that he did not belong in the classroom community.

These patterns have a logic; they are not explained solely by implicit bias or the actions of individual educators. Hazel and her handful of White peers paradoxically played the role of both the norm and the outlier at P.S. 411. Their presence served as a reference point for how children *should* be and as highly valued resources for the school's other students. School staff did not mind investing time, bending rules, or providing special services to accommodate Hazel and her family. This is unsurprising, given her status as one of the school's most valued customers. What is perhaps more unexpected is that staff appeared unaware of how unevenly their school's services, resources, and accommodations were distributed. Ultimately, rather than gaining additional resources from the presence of students like Hazel, the school diverted resources from students like Marquise. Contrary to widespread assumptions, it was the White middle-class child, rather than the Black low-income one, who benefited most from diversity.

Nancy and Janice expected very different responses from P.S. 411, and they received them. The disciplinary apparatus that seemed to unfurl almost automatically for Marquise was never even considered for Hazel. School staff met with Hazel's parents to discuss their concerns; they met with Marquise's mother to create a behavior plan. The assistant principal created a modified schedule for Hazel; she sent Marquise to in-school suspension. Staff connected Hazel's parents with an on-site therapist; they refused to evaluate Marquise for special educational services, despite Janice's request.

Rather than being deemed a problem child, Hazel was given what Diamond and Lewis have called the "silent benefit of the doubt."[27] As a result, Hazel was offered a pathway of support, counseling, and protection that was not extended to Marquise—or to the other Black children in their kindergarten class. For while Marquise's suspension was the most extreme example in K-301, he was not the only Black child whom P.S. 411 teachers labeled problematic, removed from the classroom for bad behavior, or presumed to be a victim of poor parenting.

It is particularly notable that Hazel and Marquise were treated differently in a school that was explicitly committed to treating everyone the same. Gordon Allport, writing in 1954, outlined the conditions under which contact between racial groups can reduce racial bias. The primary prerequisite, Allport argued, was "equal status" between the groups.[28] But under what circumstances can we find equal status in a deeply unequal society? Du Bois, too, wrote about the need for "contact between pupils, and between teacher and pupil, on the basis of perfect social equality."[29] However, unlike Allport, Du Bois noted that social equality is the goal, not the reality, in most settings. In fact, there is very little evidence that conditions described by equal contact theory can be achieved in schools or other organizations.[30] As the sociologists Prudence Carter and Michael Merry explain, "Equality of recognition and status would require that all children are seen to have the same intrinsic value irrespective of personal traits, cultural or socioeconomic background, or racial identity. . . . We continue to be a considerable distance from this ideal."[31] While this distance is not unique to racially and socioeconomically diverse schools, diversity does seem to heighten the gaps between ideals and reality, as well as render them particularly visible.

I do not share the story of Hazel's and Marquise's diverging reputations and the school's diverging responses as an indictment of the staff of P.S. 411. Indeed, it would be surprising if these stories had different endings; decades of anthropological research shows that we expect teachers to navigate and negotiate impossible dilemmas that are deeply woven into the fabric of our nation's racial order.[32] P.S. 411's twin goals of increasing school diversity while treating everybody "the same" were intended to increase educational equity. But as Lewis and Diamond remind us, even educators' "best intentions" cannot negate the effects of "structural inequalities, institutional practices, and racial ideologies that mutually reinforce each other but appear to be 'race-neutral.'"[33] Race shaped the school's attendance boundaries, service allocation, teacher expectations, student interactions, and staff-family relationships at P.S. 411. An approach to diversity that relied on treating everybody the same never had a chance.

3

What Is Taught and What Is Learned

Lessons from an Antiracist, Integrating Middle School

Middle School Orientation

I get off the subway and walk down the avenue behind a father and a son holding hands in the August heat. The boy looks around ten or eleven. His skin is fair, and his brown hair is cut short. I am going to sixth-grade orientation at M.S. 917, a few blocks away. As we get close to the school, I realize that they are headed there as well. I follow them through the entrance, then around the corner to the cafeteria. We see tables filled with adult and child pairs, about sixty people in all. Kids wear tee-shirts with punk rock bands and tie-dyes, cutoffs and miniskirts, baseball hats and braids, sneakers and wedge sandals. Staff wear bright-blue shirts that feature the school mascot and stand around the edges of the room. As we walk in, they hand us folders that we open eagerly, scanning information about bell schedules and emergency contact cards. I pause to say hello to Principal Myers—a White, middle-aged man with glasses—then join a table where two adult-kid duos have already settled. Soon, Principal Myers moves to the front of the room, saying "Good morning!" in a voice that does not seem all that loud but nonetheless quickly quiets the crowd.

Principal Myers smiles wryly and says that he has definitely miscalculated: one of the first things you learn as a new teacher is not to hand out materials when you need people's attention. He asks the incoming sixth graders and families to close their folders for a moment. The materials they have received, he explains, are full of details. And while people are always anxious for details at the beginning of a new school year, families can put them aside for now. Everyone there, he reminds the room, has been doing school for a long time. They can count on M.S. 917 staff to figure out the necessary logistics, but logistics are not what matters. What matters, Principal Myers reminds the room, is the reason *why* students are coming to school: "So that you can learn and understand the world in order to make it better for all of us." He pauses dramatically to deliver a message that he will return to throughout the year: "You can't do that alone." The goal for today's orientation is to prepare the students and families to do important work, "along with all the people sitting here" beside them.

After Principal Myers has finished his welcome and introduced the staff lined up alongside him, he turns his attention to the grown-ups, saying that he has a task for them: it is time to "practice saying good-bye to [their] children and sending them off to middle school." In a minute, the students will "hug and kiss their parents in front of everyone," go upstairs, and leave their families below. Adults and kids shoot each other sidewise glances as the principal urges them to give each other "real hugs" good-bye. Compliance is uneven. Kids slowly extricate their legs from the cafeteria benches and move toward the exit sign in the back corner. A few cross the room to greet each other, dapping, wrapping their arms around each other's shoulders, or hesitantly waving hi. Others studiously examine the floor. A teenager with long hair quickly walks a sixth-grade boy directly up to a teacher, saying with a bright smile, "Please take good care of my little brother!" Slowly, the group files through the door. I join the tail end of the line. We trudge up several flights of stairs, the sound of our footsteps echoing in the stairwell.

We arrive at Mr. Seif's classroom slightly out of breath. One wall is filled with posters about math facts and classroom procedures. Windows line the opposite wall, treetops visible through the sunshine. The next half hour is filled with details, just as Principal Myers had promised: introductions by each sixth-grade teacher; a slideshow with names and pictures of the administrative team and office staff; and a minute-by-minute review of the daily bell schedule. Ms. Apple, the English Language Arts (ELA) teacher, repeatedly reassures the room that all these details will feel easy after the first week. Kids look alternately skeptical and overwhelmed by this claim. As the descriptions of procedures drone on (where to find a bathroom pass, what it looks like to be prepared for class, why it is important to stay quiet in the hallways), kids lean their heads on hands propped up on their desks, gazing listlessly in front of them. They are compliant and constrained. The school year has not even started and yet there they are, doing school.

Thirty minutes later, we file out of the math room for a quick tour of the school. We visit the science, ELA, and social studies classrooms. Then we venture beyond the peninsula of the sixth-grade hallway, climbing up and down the stairs to locate the gym, art room, theater, and bathrooms. Near the school's main office, we pass a mural that shows a multiracial crowd waving protest signs; a scroll underneath the image proclaims, "Diversity Is Our Strength." Across from the mural, there is a bulletin board with a list of honor-roll students. I scan the list and see the name of a White student I recall from my first observations at M.S. 917 several years before. I am not surprised to see his name on last year's eighth-grade honor roll; in sixth grade, his teachers repeatedly commented on his reading skills and command of advanced math concepts. I wonder about the other students on the honor roll, the ones whose names I do not recognize.

We duck into a large classroom in the seventh-grade hallway, and the teachers announce that it is time to practice activities that they will use all school year in their advisory groups. Kids pass a "talking piece" around the circle as they introduce themselves. Adrianna has four brothers and two sisters; Isaac is a vegetarian; Miles and his cousin are both incoming sixth graders. Soon, they are tossing beanbags across the circle, practicing names, then sharing their hopes and fears about starting middle school. As kids articulate their anxieties, Ms. Apple reassures them that their worries are totally normal and that soon they'll feel right at home. One student raises a hand to ask if there is weekend homework at this school. A quiet sigh of relief slips around the room when Ms. Apple says that it is very rare. The group heads back to the gym to play basketball, and I slip down the hall to record my field notes from the morning.

M.S. 917, an "Antiracist, Integrated School"

I first visited M.S. 917 several years before that orientation day, during the fall that a group of White students began sixth grade there. This was a big deal; previously, the school had enrolled almost exclusively Black and Latine students. By the time I returned a couple years later for that sixth-grade orientation day, M.S. 917 was no longer "diversifying." It was racially and socioeconomically diverse: 27 percent of students that year were Black, 20 percent were Latine, 36 percent were White, and many others identified as Arab American or biracial. Just under half of the student body was eligible for free or reduced-price lunch. The group of kids I observed during orientation looked very different from the sixth graders I spent time with three years prior, when less than 5 percent of the student body had been White. However, teachers, administrators, and families often described their school as "integrating," rather than diverse or gentrifying. This integration framework distinguished M.S. 917 from P.S. 411 and many other schools.

For well over a decade, long before the 2020 Black Lives Matter protests made "antiracism" a common catchphrase, Principal Myers had demonstrated his commitment to building an antiracist school. When a small group of White, professional parents reached out about enrolling their children at M.S. 917, Principal Myers warned these families that the school would not change to accommodate their children. There would be no special programs, no treatment as valued customers. M.S. 917 had long ago eliminated academic tracks that sorted students into different classrooms according to academic ability. Instead, M.S. 917 would show what it looks like to fight racism as an integrated school. That first group of parents signed on. Soon, more White and professional families followed.

Principal Myers explained that he welcomed these "new" families to M.S. 917 in large part because they would bring much-needed material resources to the school. Like Du Bois, Principal Myers believed that "a proper education" depended on educators' professional understanding of their students' backgrounds and interests, the relationships among students and between students and teachers, and access to adequate school facilities. This last point was the impetus for integration. Principal Myers told me that "Black kids don't need to sit next to White kids to learn. There's nothing wrong with the Black kids or the Black teachers or Black administrators. There's nothing magical about the presence of White kids." However, he was confident that if more White kids attended M.S. 917, more resources would follow. Principal Myers told me, "Although people hate it—I mean, *no one* wants to acknowledge it"—he had always been sure that the school would "get more resources when there are White kids here": "They will fix the bathrooms, and change the floors, and replace the roof, and get us air conditioners." He paused, emphasizing that "people want to say that's not true anymore." But it was. As the number of White students attending M.S. 917 increased, the school did indeed receive the facilities upgrades that the principal had long requested.

Principal Myers had read extensively about the history of school integration. He knew that changing student demographics was not, in and of itself, an antiracist act; all too often, the students who benefited most from diverse schools were White. He reminded me of the various ways that integrated schools had failed their students of color, sorting them into "basic" classes and sending them to detention.[1] But still, Principal Myers pointed out, the movement for school integration had always been "solidly and clearly antiracist." He saw himself as building on that advocacy by leading a "truly" racially, economically, and academically integrated school. Because he was highly aware of his complicated position as a White man leading this work, Principal Myers deliberately cultivated what the educational leadership scholar Decoteau Irby calls the "influential presence" of faculty and administrators of color within the school community.[2] He recruited a racially diverse staff; the year I observed, sixth-grade classes were taught by two Black women, an Asian American man, two Latine women, three White women, and two White men.

As I spent the 2016–17 school year moving back and forth between M.S. 917 and P.S. 411, I often noted differences between the two schools—in particular, in the goals set by their leadership. Principal Myers did not share Principal Blake of P.S. 411's dream of a school that was "fifty-fifty" White students and students of color. He actually considered such a school segregated, given that only 18 percent of New York City students were White. When M.S. 917 became increasingly appealing to middle-class and professional White families, Principal Myers fought hard to make sure his integrated school reflected the population of the city, advocating for shifts to NYCDOE policies in order to recruit and retain more Black, Latine, and immigrant students.

Unlike Principal Blake, Principal Myers did not believe in treating everyone "the same," nor did he argue that "it doesn't matter if you're black, white, purple, or yellow." At a new staff orientation day, Principal Myers explained to the new M.S. 917 teachers that it was their responsibility to create a "level playing ground" within their classroom, "regardless of race or ethnicity or economic status." He acknowledged that this could be challenging, given the economic and racial hierarchies that students navigated outside the classroom and the different educations they had received in their segregated elementary schools. Teachers might need to provide additional support for kids who needed it most. School staff took their principal's directives seriously. While educators at P.S. 411 discussed the deficits of families and students of color, I rarely heard similar comments at M.S. 917. Neither did M.S. 917 teachers and administrators seem to see newcomers to the school as leaders or role models for their peers. Instead, they viewed White and professional families as one of many important groups of constituents.

In contrast to Principal Blake, who had explained that she was "not responsible for what happens outside" the school walls, Principal

Myers saw his work at M.S. 917 as part of a larger struggle for racial justice. In order to get staff on board with the school's mission, he devoted substantial professional development time to the long history of racism in public education. Still, he knew that some teachers and families did not share his vision. Some people, he told me, chose M.S. 917 because they wanted to be "in a diverse school, be in an antiracist school, be in an integrated school, be in an integrating school." He paused, noting that "all those things are different"; diversity is not the same as integration. But also, Principal Myers pointed out, some M.S. 917 teachers, families, and students did not think about the school's mission very much at all—they "are just here because this is where they're at." The principal saw it as his job to bring all these school community members on board for M.S. 917's ambitious goal: an integrated school that led collective work for "a just and equal society."

The Grammar of M.S. 917

Clearly, M.S. 917's educational and political values differed from those of many public schools. At the same time, the way M.S. 917 "did school" felt very familiar. As I followed sixth graders from social studies to science to the gym over the course of the school year, I repeatedly returned to the idea of "the grammar of school," which was first developed by the historians David Tyack, William Tobin, and Larry Cuban.[3] Tyack, Tobin, and Cuban argue that schools' organizational structures and routines fundamentally shape their approaches to teaching and learning. For example, it is the grammar of school that leads us to assume that elementary students will be taught by one teacher for most of the day and secondary students will be taught in a series of segmented, specialized subject-area classes; it is the grammar of school that conditions us to be surprised if children do not receive report cards with letter or numerical grades each semester. According to Tyack and Tobin, "the grammar of schooling has become so well established that it is typically taken for granted as just the way schools are."[4] Homework assignments, ability groups, and teachers lecturing at the front of the rooms form what the sociologist Jal Mehta calls the "almost invisible architecture" that holds a school together.[5] While there may be minor tweaks (perhaps students complete worksheets in groups at tables, rather than seated at individual desks), the structures and routines remain largely the same.

Departures from these practices are quite rare, in large part because they serve as a familiar container within which teachers can conduct their work. Describing the durable nature of educational routines, the historian David Labaree explains that the "most deeply entrenched school practices—the ones that have proven to be hardest to budge, like age-graded classrooms and teacher-centered instruction—strike a balance between what we want our schools to do and what those schools can realistically accomplish."[6] As a result, most schools do something closer to batch processing than teaching and learning. As Mehta asserts, the grammar of school "is designed more for efficiency and control than for learning or liberation" and shapes not just organizational structures but also classroom interactions and expectations: "They learn what we say, when we say it. Teachers dispense pre-formulated knowledge and ask questions to which they already know the answers. Students are rewarded for following directions, giving right answers, and not talking back. Students who don't fit the norm—because they are too slow, too fast, don't speak the dominant language, or resist teacher authority—are defined as problems to be fixed."[7] These assumptions, and the policies and practices that accompany them, undergird a school's hidden curriculum.

As we saw at P.S. 411, Black kids are much more likely than White kids to be categorized as problems that schools need to fix. However, scholarly analyses of the grammar of school rarely address the fact that conformity, compliance, and control are not and never can be race neutral. Education researchers have extensively documented the foundational role schools play in establishing and reinforcing both white supremacy and antiblackness.[8] Schools do not merely reproduce or reflect racial inequality; in the anthropologist Damian Sojoyner's words, they are themselves "the locus of contestation."⁹ Taken-for-granted exclusionary school discipline and academic sorting processes establish most schools as "white space," consistently and violently placing Black children at the bottom of racial and social hierarchies.[10] These patterns are neither incidental nor accidental; schools are one example or what the sociologist Victor Ray calls "racialized organizations."[11] The Black studies scholar kihana ross argues that this is part of the "afterlife of school segregation," through which "Black students remain systematically dehumanized and positioned as uneducable" long after *Brown v. Board of Education*. We therefore must "interrogate the routine and reoccurring practices of schooling that cause Black suffering, melancholy, and indignities in schooling."[12] These practices, like the organizational structures and routines that shape them, are foundational to the grammar of school.

Unlike many schools, the staff of M.S. 917 worked against the grain of their racialized organization; they did not seek to contain, control, or sort students. Principal Myers emphasized the school's focus on "teaching for understanding," rather than "compliance"—which, he pointed out, "is not necessarily the goal of American public schools." Parents received a document explaining how M.S. 917 developed students' sense of "mastery, autonomy, and accomplishment," an approach based on the principle that "building relationships with . . . students and including all of them in the community fosters engagement, keeps them safe, and increases their chances of success." When teachers talked about students' challenging behavior, Principal Myers often responded by asking them to consider, "What is getting in the way?" Staff worked extended, unpaid hours, hanging out with kids during lunch periods, before school, and after school. I watched the sixth-grade team proactively coordinate support for struggling students, arranging counseling interventions, offering legal resources for immigrant families, and supporting families as they navigated the city's homeless services. Many M.S. 917 staff considered this personalized attention, which the educational leadership scholar Rosa Rivera-McCutcheon might call "radical care," an essential part of their work.[13]

M.S. 917 staff focused on racial equity, intentionally developed supportive relationships, and considered schooling a "communal activity." Principal Myers told me that this approach had been inspired in many ways by the historical example of segregated Black schools; he emulated the commitments these community institutions made to whole child education, deep engagement with families, and providing students with the resources they deserved.[14] And so Principal Myers told sixth graders and their families during orientation that it was their job to transform the world, and he reminded staff throughout the year that it was their job to make that transformation possible. In many ways, M.S. 917 aspired to embody what the sociologist C. J. Pascoe has called "a politics of care"—a radical departure from the educational status quo, which refuses to acknowledge the systemic nature of social inequality.[15]

But fundamentally, M.S. 917 looked like . . . school. In each classroom, students filed in, sat behind desks, and turned to the teacher at the front of the room for instructions. They completed classwork and homework, copied down notes from the whiteboard, and received grades in return for their labor. If they did particularly well, they were rewarded with public recognition on the honor roll.

After I had known Principal Myers for about a year, I asked him why he did not alter the grammar of M.S. 917, given his transformative goals for the institution. His answer was illuminating. Like Mary Metz, a sociologist who studied desegregating schools in the 1970s, Principal Myers saw school norms and rituals as core elements of a common script that help us recognize a school as "real."[16] If a school is too innovative, he told me, people will not enroll—they will think "it's not school." Principal Myers did not blame those families. He did not think "people should necessarily send their kids to Walden Pond, even if Walden Pond is a really great place, when it isolates them from the work" going on outside in the real world. He explained that if he wanted families to send their children to M.S. 917, he needed to make sure they saw it as legitimate. So Principal Myers made "concessions." His goal was to make M.S. 917 as transformative as possible, given "the limitations and constructs" within which the school was working.

If Principal Myers wanted his school to appeal to a wide range of families, he had to pick and choose his battles. M.S. 917 offered an alternative to the highly segregated public educational institutions typical of New York City and the rest of the nation. Racial and economic integration provided the school crucial material resources, as well as opportunities for kids to learn about social transformation. Principal Myers refused to engage in the common practices such as academic tracking or "honors classes" that exacerbate racial and socioeconomic segregation within schools. However, he did not see eliminating grades and other markers of academic ability as a viable option. Similarly, while he repeatedly reminded staff that standardized test scores reflected student demographics, rather than actual learning, his school must administer state-mandated tests. Although M.S. 917 could push back against many aspects of neoliberal education policy, it could not completely disengage from market-based accountability reforms.

In order to be seen as a viable school choice, M.S. 917 had to conform to what the education policy scholar Elise Castillo calls "a neoliberal grammar of schooling." Castillo argues that no matter how progressive schools may aspire to be, they are situated "within a political and policy environment steeped in market values" and must therefore incorporate these values into their approaches.[17] Although Principal Myers may have rejected the basic premises of neoliberal reform, his school had to survive in a reality shaped by gentrification, school choice policy, and standards-based accountability. M.S. 917 could not afford to completely upend people's expectations if it was to remain legible in the marketplace.

What did students learn as they navigated the political commitments and institutional constraints that shaped "real school" at M.S. 917? I decided to figure this out by hanging out with one sixth-grade cohort over the course of the school year. I followed Class 6A from science to social studies to gym, chatting with students and teachers during quiet moments in the hallways. For the remainder of this chapter, we will unpack the lessons that Michelle, one socially savvy, consistently curious Black girl, learned from her integrated school that year.

In many ways, Michelle was an ideal M.S. 917 student, always eager to raise a hand, ask challenging questions, and fight racism. Her experiences at M.S. 917, like those of any student in any school, were influenced by any number of highly specific factors: her race, her gender, her likes and dislikes, her family history, and her relationships with peers and adults, to name just a few. Michelle eagerly absorbed her school's dedication to integration as a strategy for racial justice, participating in political protests and making friends across social boundaries. At the same time, her learning trajectory, like that of sixth graders across the city, was informed by the neoliberal, anti-Black grammar of school.

Introducing Michelle

> MICHELLE: I mean, some people keep their head down, and they try not to get picked on. Some people are really loud, and they walk around, and they just talk a lot. Some people always are raising their hands. Some people are always just doing something.
> ALEX: What's your way in class?
> MICHELLE: A little bit of everything. I don't really have a style yet. I'm just me.

Despite Michelle's disclaimers, she definitely had a style, a style in many ways defined by her comfort with being "just" herself. Michelle moved through M.S. 917 with notable assurance. Taller than many of her classmates, she scanned the hallways, eyes alert and ears open for interesting goings-on. It was Michelle who intervened one day when Derek, a sixth grader known to anger quickly, started arguing with another student in the hallway before math class. She stepped close to Derek and told him to take deep breaths, repeating, "You're going to be okay." Derek paused, looking into her eyes and slowing his breathing before he entered the classroom. When another student paused to gossip about the conflict,

Michelle firmly shook her head no and told the girl to move along. Michelle was powerful, in and out of class.

Like every sixth grader, Michelle was new to M.S. 917. She quickly became popular with students and teachers, who valued her verbal skills and keen sense of justice. One of the paraprofessionals who worked in Class 6A told me that everyone liked Michelle because she was "not afraid to voice her opinion." Even from the first week of school, she explained, Michelle could be counted on to "stand up for what's right and wrong." Students and staff alike appreciated her conviction and her influence over others. Nobody thought Michelle was perfect. Kids vented about her "bossy" attitude; adults were frustrated by her dramatic eye rolls and "incessant" talking during class. Still, her classmates wanted to work with her in group projects because, as one classmate explained, "she, like, brings the fun, and she also helps us stay focused." Everyone seemed to admire Michelle, even as they sometimes chafed at her assertive behavior or her lack of compliance with school norms.

Teachers were impressed (and at times irritated) by Michelle's influence over her classmates. Her authority was so widely recognized that occasionally it became part of the formal curriculum, reflecting the ways in which classroom learning, student identity, and social power often intertwine, as the anthropologist Stanton Wortham has demonstrated.[18] One day in February, for example, sixth graders were learning a lesson about tyranny as part of their study of Ancient Greece. Mr. Tello, a White man who had taught social studies for several years, explained that the word "tyrant" was originally used for "anybody who came to power in an unconventional way." The term did not have to be negative, as it is now. Mr. Tello looked around at the sixth graders seated before him at square tables: "Let's say a powerful, influential student, maybe like Michelle, says, 'These teachers aren't looking out for students' interests.'" Expanding on this hypothetical, Mr. Tello wove a narrative in which Michelle made a bid to overthrow the M.S. 917 faculty. Michelle sat straight up in her seat, immediately denying that she would ever do such a thing, while struggling to hide a smile. She appreciated the public recognition of her leadership, but she also seemed concerned by Mr. Tello's premise that she would rebel against authority. Mr. Tello continued his story: "She promises no homework ever and free time on all the laptops. . . . She says, 'Trust me!'" Sixth graders, delighted by this scenario, clamored from their desks. Over their exclamations, Mr. Tello explained that Michelle's first step would be to "kick out the people in power" with "popular support" because that is what tyrants do. At this point, Michelle decided to play along, exclaiming with a grin that she would not just help sixth graders—she would bring in the seventh and eighth graders too! After all, it would not be fair to get rid of just *some* of the teachers.

I watched the back and forth from my seat at Michelle's table, entertained. Unable to resist my impulse to join in, I quietly urged her to ask Mr. Tello what usually happens to tyrants. Michelle's eyes widened. She quickly turned back to Mr. Tello and asked, "Isn't it possible I can get overthrown?" Mr. Tello nodded, "Absolutely!" He explained that tyrants usually get comfortable: "Maybe you would decide the laptops are just for my friends and me." As Michelle shook her head vigorously, he went on, "Soon Elijah is saying, 'You can't trust Michelle anymore!' . . . Then Christopher says, 'Let's all relax. We're going to have a vote.' And everyone says, 'Christopher, that's a good idea.'" Michelle loudly mourned the loss of her title as the students of Class 6A howled with laughter. Together, they had learned a new lesson about more than systems of government—they had learned about social and political power, inside and outside the classroom. Through repeated exposure over the course of the school year, Michelle and her peers mastered three such lessons.

Lesson One: Integrated Schools Can Fight Racism

M.S. 917 staff often reminded sixth graders that the school's success depended on their joint efforts. They hoped M.S. 917 would serve as a model of not just a diverse school but an integrated, antiracist school. Michelle believed deeply in this goal.

When I asked Michelle to describe the most important difference she noticed between M.S. 917 and her elementary school, she looked at me gravely and said that "there were some very racist people" at her previous school. Michelle detailed a series of "little incidents" and classroom bullies, such as a White girl who demanded her art materials, saying, "I'm better than you." In that school, she explained, "there were some teachers who would separate us, White and Black. . . . If the kids who they would put in the White group say that they did something wrong, the teachers would brush it off. But the teachers, if we were in the colored group, if we did something, they would call our parents. They would call us the bad children. They would tell the next teacher we would have next year; they would warn them about us." Startled by the mention of segregation, I asked Michelle to clarify: were Black and White children seated apart? "No," she said, "but it just felt like that, the way they were kind of doing, how they were treating us." Michelle and I sat together for a moment in silence, considering that pattern.

But at M.S. 917, things were different. At Michelle's old school, "you weren't able to express who you were without somebody looking bad on you or saying that it was not okay." At M.S. 917, Michelle explained, "they try to put you together instead of separating you." Michelle was sure that racial diversity alone was not what made M.S. 917 unique. After all, her previous school had included both Black and White students, and she had seen what happened there. When I asked Michelle what made this school so different, she thought for a moment and then replied, "The principal maybe. The principal focuses a lot on racism and how we can stop it." Principal Myer's efforts to make the school antiracist mattered, in part, because they allowed Michelle to develop a new relationship with school. She told me that at M.S. 917, "they just want it to be as equal as possible."

But it was not always simple. On the one hand, Michelle's friendship group included Black, Latine, and White students. On the other hand, Michelle explained that during lunchtime, "we split into different groups. We go—some people don't notice it, but we kind of go into our colored groups." Michelle paused, saying that she was not quite sure how to explain this pattern. Then she continued, "We separate into those groups, but then eventually we will mix it up. Like, when it's time for lunch, there'll be a group of African Americans over here. There'll be Spanish kids over here.... Then after we've eaten and talked with our groups, we'll get up and walk around and just mix it up." Of course, Michelle was not the first person to notice this phenomenon. The psychologist Beverly Daniel Tatum famously wrote a book titled *Why Are All the Black Kids Sitting Together in the Cafeteria?*, and other scholars have examined the role that racial identity plays in student friendships.[19] However, Michelle's careful observation of these trends indicated how important she considered the goal of integration. A moment after telling me about sixth graders' informal lunchtime racial affinity groups, Michelle backed up to clarify, "I don't mind... as long as we're all socializing at one point." Her analysis demonstrated a sophisticated awareness of interpersonal and broader social dynamics: she saw cross-racial friendships as a goal worth pursuing; she simultaneously recognized that there might be obstacles to these relationships, and she felt like it was understandable to want to spend part of lunchtime with people like yourself.

In a study of multiracial schools in the United States and South Africa, the sociologist Prudence Carter found that the students who were most likely to develop cultural flexibility attended majority-minority schools where they felt safe and secure, were placed in untracked classrooms, and were actively encouraged to broaden their cultural horizons.[20] These schools based their policies and practices on the moral conditions of equity, caring, and sharing. M.S. 917, with its intentionally majority-minority student body and explicit commitment to antiracist education, exceeded these criteria in several ways. Not just during lunch but also during class time, M.S. 917 students worked together to develop their communication skills. Michelle was a leader in this arena as well. Early in the school year, Mr. Tello described Michelle to me as a "gap-bridger," someone who is "just more at ease talking to people that we would think of as different from them." He believed kids like Michelle who had strong listening and speaking skills "are really good in a group like this because they're more patient, they're open to new ideas, they're comfortable with themselves, so they're less judgmental of others." These are hallmarks of cultural flexibility.

M.S. 917 students had multiple opportunities to practice the cross-cultural communication skills that many families and educators deeply value. As Carter explains, racially diverse, resource-rich schools like M.S. 917 offer the chance to teach students to "conceive of themselves as multifaceted cultural beings" who can interact appropriately and effectively in multiple cultural settings.[21] However, advocates who focus primarily on what students learn from diversity may fail to recognize that cultural flexibility is not the same as antiracism. As the Black studies scholar Michael Dumas has demonstrated, diversity can coexist with—in fact, it often relies on—antiblackness.[22]

M.S. 917 aspired to be integrated and antiracist, not merely diverse. This goal was particularly evident during Black History Month. During the month of February, schools across the country hold assemblies that feature biographies of Black leaders, films about the civil rights movement, and celebrations of Black excellence. M.S. 917's Black History Month celebration both was and was not very different. When sixth graders filed downstairs into the school's theater for their first Black History Month assembly, they entered a room filled with seats covered in red velvet, a spotlight shining on a lofted stage, and murals and decorative carvings covering the walls. At first, they called raucously across the audience, saying hi to friends from other classrooms. But soon, the house lighting went down, the curtain went up, and students turned their attention to the stage.

The assembly began with the students' friends and classmates. The audience cheered as a trio of Black girls sang and danced to spirituals, accompanied by three drummers. Sixth graders performed "Lift Ev'ry Voice and Sing" (also known as the "Black National Anthem") and the South African national anthem, which they had learned in chorus at the beginning of the school year. Then, Principal Myers welcomed the school to the celebration, explaining that this year's assembly theme was "using multiracial unity to fight racism and inequality." Kid chatter slowly swelled as social studies teachers shared PowerPoint presentations about Bacon's Rebellion and the Spanish Civil War, but attention quickly returned to the stage when it was time to watch a video made by eighth graders. Mr. Tello, the sixth grade social studies teacher, had told me that morning in a slightly awed tone that the eighth-grade teachers "stopped all curriculum" so their class could research, write, rehearse, and produce a movie about the Underground Railroad. The ten-minute video told the story of a girl who goes back in time and joins the resistance. Sixth graders hollered their appreciation over the applause as the final credits rolled.

The assembly closed with several student speakers who shared an update about M.S. 917 graduates who were recently the targets of racist attacks. The school was working on a response. As kids stood up to go back to classes, murmuring in dismay, an adult shouted out in ringing tones, "An injustice to one!" Quickly, the audience responded, "An injustice to all!" Eighth graders were practiced in the rituals of protest. Sixth graders quickly caught on and joined in. The call and response continued as the students filed out the theater doors to return to class.

Later that day, Angela, one of Michelle's White classmates, told me how exciting she found the assembly; she liked knowing that people can "make changes in the world." She was not alone. At the end of the year, I asked a group of sixth graders what made M.S. 917 different from other schools. They rushed to explain to me that *their* school was "trying to fight against racism." M.S. 917 sixth graders learned that schools have political values and that those values matter, for their students and for their community. They knew that school could be more than a place where you make friends; it could also be a place where you learn to protest and where assemblies teach you about the power of multiracial unity. Their principal talked about how to fight racism, their teachers were committed to integration, and they learned in community with people very unlike themselves. At M.S. 917, students learned that one goal of education was to fight for racial justice.

Lesson Two: We Don't Talk about Race in Class

Although Michelle learned about activism in assemblies and analyzed seating patterns in the M.S. 917 lunchroom, her classes tended to avoid discussions of racial injustice and antiracism. Because sixth-grade courses adhered closely to New York State standards, lessons frequently sidelined student ideas and questions that could have played a central role in M.S. 917's work as an integrated, antiracist school. These patterns demonstrated the limits of standardized approaches to curriculum and instruction.

For example, the sixth-grade social studies curriculum examined ancient civilizations. Mr. Tello was very interested in teaching his classes about social and political power. However, he was also reluctant to deviate from his lesson plans. One day during a unit about Mesopotamia, Michelle raised an eyebrow, noting the description of slaves who were buried in the queen's tomb, and told her table group, "I don't like slavery in general." When nobody responded, Michelle sat and waited until Mr. Tello had finished reading a poem about a goddess out loud. Then she asked, "Did *she* have slaves?" Mr. Tello paused. He explained that goddesses did not have human slaves and then noted, "You've got your eye on this. You're always on the lookout for the question of slaves." Michelle confirmed his observation: "I am. Because I'm not cool with someone who has slaves." Mr. Tello nodded, turning to the class to ask them to start writing down their homework. He crossed the room to Michelle to continue their conversation, so quietly that I could not hear from the table next to her. Michelle's persistence eventually received a response. However, her teacher's focus on moving through instructional materials foreclosed an opportunity for the entire class to collectively learn about race and social power.

Another day in the social studies class, during an introduction to the ancient Egyptian caste system, Michelle urgently waved her hand after another student made a comment about pharaohs being at the top of the social pyramid. She wanted to know if there had ever been an African American pharaoh. Mr. Tello explained that the pharaoh could not be African American, since the United States did not exist yet, but that "the pharaohs *were* African, since Egypt is in Africa." Michelle quietly nodded. Jayden, a Black boy sitting across the room, asked a confused question: Why were the pharaohs so "pale" if they were in Africa? Mr. Tello paused and said, "Well, they weren't, but that's a really interesting question. Why do we represent them that way?" Jayden, Michelle, and several other Black students looked up at their teacher, waiting for an answer. They did not receive one. Mr. Tello returned to his main lesson, guiding students through the notes he had prepared about the Egyptian caste system.

It did not have to be this way. The curriculum scholar Gloria Ladson-Billings, in her landmark work on culturally relevant pedagogy (CRP), has argued that effective teachers of African American students focus not only on student learning but also on cultural competence (which is similar to Carter's concept of cultural flexibility) and critical consciousness (which is similar to Paulo Freire's theory of engaging critically with the written word and the social world).[23] Although the catchphrase "CRP" has been widely adopted over the past few decades, Ladson-Billings charges that it is often distorted.[24] Accountability-based reforms conflate standardized test scores with learning and influence educators to ignore critical consciousness altogether.[25] The neoliberal, anti-Black grammar of school subverts what Ladson-Billings has called CRP's central goal: using classroom curriculum and instruction to refute white supremacy. This was a vision of educational transformation that Principal Myers shared but that his staff rarely actualized.

This pattern became particularly clear in November 2016, the week that Donald Trump was elected president. The day after the election, many sixth-grade teachers worried deeply about the potential impact on students who had undocumented family members or whose families had experienced police violence. School staff came in early and stayed late that Wednesday, talking quietly and urgently with students; they made careful plans for supportive conversations in advisory groups later that week. Very early in the morning, Principal Myers had emailed teachers several texts they might want to read and discuss in class that day, including Martin Luther King Jr.'s "Letter from a Birmingham Jail." However, none of the sixth-grade teachers took him up on that suggestion. Ms. Apple, the ELA teacher, told me at the time that she could not imagine how to fit the text into the unit plan she had developed. Since she was teaching persuasive writing, I asked if she could use "Letter from a Birmingham Jail" as an example in class. Ms. Apple shook her head—she was not ready to change the lesson plans she had already prepared for the week. Instead, she would address the events with her advisory group in a few days.

Ms. Apple did, indeed, talk about the election with students in her advisory that Friday. Kids shared their concerns about undocumented family members who would not be able to get home under President Trump's immigration policies; their friends listened, offered support, and learned with Ms. Apple's help.[26] When the Trump administration severely limited immigration a few months later, teachers invited sixth graders to spend an advisory period making protest posters that they could use, if they wished, during a rally that was held off-campus after the school day had ended. However, classroom lessons only rarely referred to the political conversations teachers had with students in extracurricular spaces. Despite all the work going on in advisories, Black History Month assemblies, and orientation sessions, instruction at M.S. 917 looked very much like that at many New York City middle schools.

There were exceptions to this trend. In chorus, kids analyzed the similarities and differences between "The Star-Spangled Banner," the South African national anthem, and "Lift Ev'ry Voice and Sing." The class talked about Colin Kaepernick's decision to kneel during the national anthem in protest of police brutality and analyzed the different ways that people can use song as social protest. However, chorus was an elective course and therefore considered less "academic" than ELA or science; as such, curricular standards were perceived as more flexible and lower stakes. In contrast, when students asked related questions about racial injustice in their "core academic classes," teachers rarely took up these bids, despite encouragement from Principal Myers to do so.

Many M.S. 917 staff had carefully developed what Du Bois called "knowledge on the part of the teacher, not simply of the individual taught, but of his surroundings and background, and the history of his class and group."[27] They paid careful attention to students' individual and collective experiences. However, they did not consistently connect that knowledge to classroom teaching and learning. While they got to know students well and offered substantial individual support, their instructional approaches were often quite rigid. I rarely observed a teacher adapting lesson plans on the fly or deviating from state-mandated curricular standards.

Principal Myers gave M.S. 917 faculty a great deal of freedom. He trusted them to do the right thing, telling them he would support them as long as they kept students at the center of their decisions. However, many teachers appeared not to know *how* to teach in other ways. Nor did they seem to recognize the role that culturally relevant pedagogy might play in building an antiracist, integrated school. Recall Mr. Tello's wondering words about the Black History Month assembly: the eighth grade had "stopped all curriculum" to create a project about the Underground Railroad.

During new staff orientation, Principal Myers told incoming teachers, "Our philosophy is that this is a profession. You all are professionals. It's a hard job. Teaching and learning *is* rocket science. Actually, it's harder than rocket science." However, over the past two decades of education reform, teachers' work has been increasingly deprofessionalized; with few exceptions, their preservice training and professional experience has been limited to centralized standards and accountability-based reforms.[28] While Principal Myers emphasized "teaching for understanding" and consistently denounced reliance on standardized tests, he did not devote significant professional development time to classroom pedagogy. None of the sixth-grade teachers at M.S. 917 had more than five years' experience in the classroom. Principal Myers, trained in a different context, may not have fully recognized the extent to which recent reforms have limited teachers' experience with critical pedagogical approaches. He might not have predicted that Mr. Tello would perceive making a class film about the Underground Railroad as "stopping" curriculum.

That sixth-grade teachers rarely deviated from the grammar of standardized curriculum and instruction is not necessarily surprising. As Metz wrote in 1989, in "real school," the vast majority of teachers "did not expect to tailor the institution or the learning to the students, but assumed that they must tailor the students to the institution."[29] These expectations were probably augmented by the demands of standards-based accountability reforms. These neoliberal policies made the grammar of schooling—always quite rigid—even more restrictive and standardized.

In Pauline Lipman's words, neoliberal approaches to education have serious implications for "the moral and intellectual life of teachers and students."[30] In a study of how accountability-based reforms influenced teachers' professional knowledge, Jessica Holloway and Jory Brass found that during the initial years following the passage of No Child Left Behind, teachers remained confident that their experience and knowledge of their students qualified them "to know what and how to teach, as well as when was the most appropriate time and methods for their respective students," regardless of the dictates of state-mandated standards. A decade later, however, "the distance between the teachers and the accountability apparatus" had "all but collapsed"; teachers were more likely to consider themselves "transmitters of pre-determined standards and the ones responsible for delivering content correctly and objectively."[31] As the historians Camika Royal and Simone Gibson argue, neoliberal reforms "standardize and homogenize" curriculum and teacher preparation, leaving little room for "creativity, divergent thinking, problem-solving, and resistance" among either teachers or students.[32] In Ladson-Billings's words, many teachers no longer understand "their pedagogy as art—unpredictable, always in the process of becoming."[33]

Michelle's sixth-grade year demonstrated that it takes significant instructional skill and experience for teachers to effectively bridge gaps between state-mandated curricula and students' pressing questions about racial injustice and antiracism. Many M.S. 917 staff did not achieve or even articulate this goal. The school did not intend to replicate the instructional status quo, but educators did not appear to know how to do otherwise.

Lesson Three: It's Unusual for Black Kids to Get Good Grades

Adults and kids at M.S. 917 repeatedly encountered a troubling question: Why did White kids at their antiracist school almost always get the best grades? In Michelle's class, for example, there were only eight White kids out of twenty-five total students. However, almost all the kids on the honor roll who came from that cohort were White. Although this pattern is extremely disturbing, it is not necessarily surprising: educational researchers have documented decades-long trends of racialized success and failure, even in schools committed to racial equity.[34]

Some M.S. 917 students responded to this pattern by denying it. At the end of the school year, I asked a group of sixth graders how they would think about a school where only 20 percent of the kids were White, but the honor roll included mostly White students. Kids immediately gasped, saying, "Oh my God! No! It's crazy!" One White boy told me that something like this could *never* happen at M.S. 917; he pointed to the only Black sixth grader who consistently held a spot on the M.S. 917 honor roll as evidence for his claim. Others cried out that it was "shady" or that they would start a "riot" if they went to a school like that. As a group, they agreed that such a school must be racist. At no point did they acknowledge that the achievement patterns at this hypothetical school were similar to those at M.S. 917, where only 36 percent of students were White but almost all the honor roll students were White.

Michelle was not in the room during that conversation. She was, however, one of only three Black students whose names periodically appeared on the sixth-grade honor roll over the course of the year. In our interview, Michelle told me about a school-wide honor-roll breakfast: "I and another kid were the only two African Americans there, and then it was just Whites. . . . It wasn't pleasant." She explained, her voice carefully even, perhaps resigned, "I've been trying to prove myself to see, to show that I'm just as good as them because, since the beginning of the school year, I was on the honor roll. But it's just hard to keep trying to prove yourself to them. Even if I get on the honor roll again, I wouldn't care. It'd just be another thing saying that, 'Okay. This one is just now coming up to our level.'" I asked Michelle if not caring meant that she was going to give up on her grades. She explained that even though the honor-roll breakfast had not been pleasant, it still "felt good to be like, 'You see, I'm African American, and I can do it, but I don't want to do it for you guys. I want to do it for myself.'" I wondered who "you guys" were, exactly. Who was Michelle showing? Her teachers? I asked her, and she clarified that "you guys" was a broader audience of people who were always watching: "The people who still believe in racism and the people who still believe that Blacks are not superior to Whites." Michelle felt very sure that her teachers were not among "those people," since she knew that M.S. 917 was an antiracist school. However, she felt equally sure that nobody other than her mother and herself had cared that there were only two Black kids at the honor-roll breakfast, given that the school never acknowledged this pattern.

Public recognition of academic ability matters—that is why schools have honor rolls. It was important to Michelle that others see her as smart. When I asked her how other students might describe her, she replied, "goofy and intelligent, but she chooses not to show it." She told me that she did not want her friends to know that she struggled with her grades, because "it's just not something you want to share, just go up to your friend and be like, 'Hey, I'm failing. Can you help me?' That's not something you want to tell your friend." She wanted to be known as someone who could succeed on her own, if she made the choice to do so. As a result, Michelle had to constantly negotiate her own expectations of herself and others' expectations of her. Classmates assumed Michelle would offer, not receive, help. Yet at several points during sixth grade, teachers called Michelle's mother to warn that her grades were in serious danger. That winter, I sat in on several conversations in which teachers worried aloud about her resistance to turning in assignments. Michelle got an 80 percent for English Language Arts that marking period. It was not a term where she was on the honor roll.

According to Michelle, grades were not a reflection of her intelligence or her learning, even if other people might think they were. In fact, when I asked Michelle if her grades increased when she was learning more, she shrugged, "I don't know. I never really thought of that." What she did think about frequently was the point in the school year when her "grades were kind of going deep down in the ocean" and she "had to find a way to swim to the top." Michelle did extra credit and began checking the school's computerized progress reports. Still, she explained, it was hard to keep it up: "I've been doing that for a really long time, and I just got tired of it." Perhaps as a result, Michelle's grades waxed and waned over the course of the school year as she actively managed relationships with her friends and teachers, distinctions between grades and learning, and competing desires to prove her intelligence and to allow herself space to be "tired." As I watched Michelle negotiate these interactions and expectations, I wondered what they cost her.

During conversations about Michelle, teachers frequently commented on her refusal to stay quiet and comply with racialized and gendered classroom norms. Over the course of the school year, Mr. Seif zigzagged Michelle's seat assignment back and forth across the math classroom in an attempt to isolate her from "chitchat." Many M.S. 917 staff admired Michelle's boldness and willingness to challenge authority. M.S. 917—unlike many other schools—explicitly celebrated Black girlhood in moments such as the Black History Month assembly.[35] And yet still, staff felt the need to address what the anthropologist Savannah

Shange, writing about educators and students in another politically progressive, racially diverse school, described as "unruly blackness."[36] Like many other Black girls, Michelle was taught to see herself as in need of discipline in order to succeed.

The racialized patterns I observed at M.S. 917 were not particularly unusual. They were, however, more visible than in most segregated New York City schools, due to the school's racial diversity. Grades, like many of schools' organizational routines, are often assumed to be racially neutral reflections of individual effort. However, it simply is not possible for them to play that role. As the anthropologist Thea Abu El-Haj writes, "academic success and failure are co-constructed through relationships between students, teachers, curriculum, and pedagogy."[37] However, standardized grading policies and practices measure youth of color by what Django Paris and Sami Ali call the yardstick of "white middle-class norms of knowing and being."[38] An expansive body of literature shows that teachers' unconscious racialized perceptions play an important role in assessments of students' ability.[39] The assignment of students to positions on or off the honor roll teaches students about not only their achievement but also their potential.

At the end of the school year, I tentatively asked Principal Myers what he thought about the M.S. 917 honor roll. With a sigh, Principal Myers told me that if a racially representative honor roll were the only indicator that M.S. 917 had reached its antiracist goals, the school was bound to fail. He explained with evident regret that he did not expect the demographics to change anytime soon; structural inequality and significant differences in family resources and prior schooling played central roles in students' academic outcomes. But, Principal Myers pointed out, a diverse honor roll was not his only goal. I asked the obvious question: What *were* the principal's other goals for M.S. 917? He shrugged and said, "Well, partly to understand how stupid grades and test scores are, which is really hard, because we can't get rid of them." Principal Myers explained that to get rid of the "frigging honor roll" would be impossible, because without grades and an honor roll, "we won't be a school."

The fact that Principal Myers did not abolish the honor roll despite his conviction that grades are "stupid" illustrates how difficult it is to change specific aspects of schooling without altering its fundamental norms, routines, and structures. Grades play a central role in the grammar of school; they are understood to measure productivity, compliance, and (at times) mastery of specific academic skills and knowledge. Although Principal Myers recognized the ways grades are used to label and sort children and although he knew that the resulting academic hierarchy almost invariably places Black children and immigrant children of color at the bottom, he also saw that families needed grades to recognize M.S. 917 as a "real school." The honor roll was one of the "concessions" he made to the educational marketplace.

Michelle—always asking challenging questions, consistently refusing to accept inadequate responses—was also highly aware of the ways that grades both do and do not matter. She knew that her name on the honor roll did not necessarily demonstrate meaningful learning. Yet Michelle was also exhausted and angered by the fact that in her integrated school, Black kids rarely managed to "swim to the top."

The Neoliberal, Anti-Black Grammar of School

Summer approached. Classroom windows were opened wide to let in fresh air as the days grew warmer and sixth graders edged closer to puberty. By now, Michelle was just one of many students who eagerly raised her hand during class discussions. Ms. Apple sent students out into the hallway to work unsupervised, confident that they knew what they needed to do. One day in May, Mr. Tello touched base with me after class. With great pride, he listed all the students who had shared ideas that day, including kids who had historically been extremely reluctant to work in small groups. "I guess they learned this year," he said with a smile, and then, looking more serious, he added, "They couldn't have done this at the beginning of the year."

The lessons Michelle and her classmates learned in sixth grade went broad and deep. As the sociologist Margaret Hagerman argues, middle childhood is a period in which young people produce ideological positions related to race and politics, positions that they become increasingly committed to as they grow older.[40] M.S. 917 students were likely to remember how their school taught them to fight for racial justice. Michelle never doubted that her principal and her teachers cared deeply about and believed in her. These experiences differed starkly from those of Black students in many schools.[41] Yet as Dumas reminds us, all too often "racial justice discourse in education proceeds past/around/on the back of Black suffering, rendering Black suffering invisible or beside the point, and, most pointedly, inconsequential."[42] Michelle's exhaustion and anger—her suffering—was deeply consequential, for herself, for her classmates, and for her school.

M.S. 917 aspired to be different from other schools. Under the leadership of Principal Myers, the school reached beyond diversity, toward a transformative vision of integration.[43] The values the staff embraced and the actions they took played a central role in teaching students how to resist racial inequality; the welcome speeches at orientation, the chants at Black History Month assemblies, and the supportive circles in advisory periods were testimony to the school's politics of care. At the same time, classroom practices and school routines told and retold status quo stories that reinscribed narratives of individual merit and collective deficit. The teachers assigning grades and standing in front of whiteboards often contributed to racial inequality in their classrooms, despite their determination to do otherwise. Although teachers strove to shift racialized patterns, their success depended on more than their individual effort. The school's hidden curriculum was invisibly structured by the neoliberal, anti-Black grammar of school.

As Principal Myers told me, "It's limited, what our hopes and desires and even conscious effort can do, you know, in any one particular school." Constraints, by definition, constrain.[44] The lessons M.S. 917

sixth graders learned were the outcomes of *both* intentional antiracist work *and* neoliberal, anti-Black school policies and practices. Many of these lessons are not particular to "diverse" or "integrating" schools; after all, durable patterns of racial inequality and antiblackness have been widely documented in decades of educational research. Nor are the challenges involved in developing culturally responsive curricula and instruction specific to neoliberal contexts, although they have been exacerbated by standardized approaches.[45] Still, the stubborn persistence of these practices and outcomes in a school explicitly dedicated to fighting racism—a school that took many significant steps toward racial justice—is notable.

There was a significant distance between the political and pedagogical approaches that M.S. 917 adopted. Adults and kids alike learned from the gaps between the Black History Month assembly and the sixth-grade social studies curricula, from teachers' persistent failure to answer students' pressing questions about racial injustice, and from the racial hierarchy of the honor roll. These patterns vividly illustrate the ways that neoliberal education policies such as school choice and standards-based reforms compound long-standing antiblackness in public schools.

The Limits and Opportunities of Integration

M.S. 917 offers us important lessons in both the limits and opportunities that school integration offers as a strategy for racial justice. Sixth graders at M.S. 917 learned not just from what they were taught explicitly but also from school norms and practices, which were in turn shaped by the surrounding policy environment. If we wish students to learn from their diverse classrooms, we must prepare educators to approach their work as improvisational, rather than a set of scripted "best practices" for which teachers and schools will be held accountable.[46] As the curriculum scholars Na'ilah Nasir, Maxine McKinney de Royston, and their colleagues write, "systems of oppression are not separate from processes of learning that occur within these systems."⁴⁷ You cannot clean the air on one side of a screen door.

The durable nature of racial inequality in a school dedicated to fighting injustice can and should make us uncomfortable. Unlike many educators, M.S. 917 teachers and staff did not focus on "nice" approaches to diversity, nor did they strive to treat all their students the same.⁴⁸ The disjuncture between M.S. 917's goals and practices raises urgent questions: Is it possible for a school to be antiracist within a system predicated on antiblackness? Is it possible for a school to offer new ways of seeing the world without shifting the neoliberal grammar of schooling?

I do not ask these questions to minimize M.S. 917's accomplishments. As I sat in classrooms and walked through the corridors of the school, I periodically thought how fortunate I would be to send my own (White) kids there. I believe my children would absorb more of the lessons I want them to learn at M.S. 917 than they would in almost any other school. However, in those same spaces, I reflected on what Shange describes as the "late liberal double bind: we work for institutions that we know are soaked in bias and inequity, even as we know those same institutions have (more or less) robust commitments to ending bias and inequity."⁴⁹

Together, M.S. 917 staff and students envisioned new purposes for a "real school": to engage in struggle for racial justice, while engaging in meaningful learning across racial boundaries. The persistence of status quo approaches to school and classroom practice in the context of these transformative objectives pushes us to reconsider the ends and means of both neoliberal reform and school integration. As Tyack and Tobin argue, if we aspire to more ambitious educational goals, we need "intense and continual public dialogue about the ends and means of schooling, including cultural assumptions about what a 'real school' is."⁵⁰ Du Bois demands that we focus on the actual lessons students learn from diversity, even in schools as caring and committed as M.S. 917.

After I had completed an early draft of this chapter, I asked Principal Myers to read it and offer some feedback. His response was exceedingly generous; he shared pages of notes and a lengthy reflection describing his understanding of how integration can "push the limits of public education." I found his argument powerful; I did indeed see M.S. 917 pushing the limits of the New York City school system. However, I also saw Michelle's experience as indicative of the intractable nature of those limits. M.S. 917 demonstrates the constraints of school integration as a strategy for advancing racial justice—even as it underscores the urgency of continuing to work toward that goal.

All year long, I watched Michelle deliberate over when and how to take up, adapt, and resist the various lessons M.S. 917 offered her. Her experiences raise important questions about what it means to treat kids not just as students, not just as learners, but as policy actors. Michelle chose when to press her questions in class and when to let them go, when to pursue the honor roll and when to abandon that goal, when to hang out with other Black kids in the cafeteria and when to "mix it up." In doing so, she influenced more than her own individual trajectory; Michelle's actions and reactions illustrate the powerful roles that students, as well as educators, can play in shaping educational policy. This is a possibility that we will examine in greater depth in chapter 4.

4

"A True History of America"

Civic Learning through Youth Organizing for School Integration

The longer I stayed in Teens Take Charge, the more educated I got, the more educated I got in not just school segregation in New York City, in America, but also just a true history of America. School didn't teach me about Black history, and school didn't teach me about what America truly did to Black people in America. And so, Teens Take Charge is where I learned it.
—Maimouna, Black, junior

On a practical level, I've understood more about the way government works and how to be a responsible citizen in the future. I mean, I always knew, like, I'm gonna register to vote. Executive, legislative, judicial, I knew the three branches of government or whatever. But Teens Take Charge is the best civics class I could've ever gotten. I didn't understand how much power our city council has or who does what at the DOE, and I just—I've learned practical things that I should have been learning in school from the time I was younger, but I didn't. And now I've learned about them from such a hands-on way. It's like, you know, I don't just know what happens in City Hall. I've been *in* the meetings in City Hall.
—Margot, White, senior

Margot and Maimouna were both high school students. They were also both youth leaders at Teens Take Charge (TTC), which they described as a student-led organization that fought for integration and educational equity in the New York City public school system. Their work at Teens Take Charge involved meeting with local politicians, organizing public protests, parsing the details of educational policy, and mastering the history of school segregation in New York City. As they mapped and navigated the New York City policy landscape, youth leaders developed a sense of agency in a system that positioned them as policy targets, rather than policy actors. Along the way, they learned overlapping yet diverging lessons about race, inequality, and civic change.

Teens Take Charge was a very different learning environment from the public schools that members attended. Unlike New York's segregated high schools, Teens Take Charge included young people with a wide range of racial, cultural, linguistic, socioeconomic, and academic experiences. As members worked together to change education policy, they grappled with inequalities within the group. Their individual and collective trajectories show us what integration can and cannot offer people fighting for just educational policy—in a space led by teenagers, outside the grammar of school.

Like M.S. 917, Teens Take Charge was a highly diverse organization working toward educational justice. Unlike M.S. 917, the group's hidden curriculum was not shaped by state-mandated standards or school choice policies. However, that did not mean that Teens Take Charge operated without constraints. As the sociologist Bianca Baldridge has demonstrated, community-based youth organizations—often portrayed as "places of refuge" in which young people can reflect critically on their experiences in school and society—are increasingly undermined by market-based approaches to education.[1] In particular, the Asian American studies scholar Soo Ah Kwon argues that most youth organizing programs, like "civil society writ large, are intricately enmeshed in the neoliberal state."[2] However, their enmeshment looks very different from that of the public school system, which is a direct arm of the state. By examining informal learning environments such as Teens Take Charge, we can see what kinds of learning from integration are and are not available beyond the boundaries of the formal educational system.

This chapter examines what Teens Take Charge members learned from their fight for equitable education policy in New York City. We begin by situating the group's activism within the broader landscape of youth organizing. Then, we identify the crucial roles that the elements of choice, peer teaching, and collective labor toward a shared, urgent goal—elements often absent from school classrooms—played in the group's learning environment. Finally, we analyze how racial diversity both strengthened and complicated the organization's efforts. Teens Take Charge members' understandings of structural inequality, the purpose of integration, and the nature of public policy varied widely, often along racial lines. Attending to these differences offers a new lens on the hidden curriculum of school integration.

"Well, Now I'm Angry!": Organizing High School Students against School Segregation

Teens Take Charge was founded in 2016 by the high school students Nelson Luna and Whitney Stephenson, with the support of Taylor McGraw, a podcaster and former teacher. Taylor (who is White) met Nelson (who is Latine) and Whitney (who is Black) when he visited their charter high school for his podcast on New York City schools. At some point in the day, Taylor asked Nelson and Whitney if they had any White friends. They were dismayed to realize that not only did they not have White friends but they did not *know* any White kids. Both Nelson and Whitney were poets and had many friends who also did spoken word; Taylor helped them organize an event about how they experienced school segregation. One event led to another and then another, in which small groups of high school students shared public testimony about their segregated schools.

Over time, the group's focus shifted from public storytelling to political advocacy. Margot, a White youth leader, described this new focus as almost inevitable: "Once you hear everyone's stories, it's like, 'Well, now I'm angry! What can I do about it?' So, then there was a big shift to more policy work." Soon, a group of young people from schools across the city was advocating for equitable and integrated high school admission policies. Along the way, Teens Take Charge developed a reputation for relentless, even slightly radical, criticism of City Hall. In the words of a youth leader, the group did whatever it took to draw attention to their cause:

> We talk to people one on one. We do social media kind of outreach. We go into schools and talk to kids. We have partner organizations. We do outreach to get people to show up to actions, to do actions and join us kind of all along the way. And so, you know, one action we did was a demonstration on the steps of City Hall, and then when that didn't lead to policy change, we decided to scale it up. So we did a sit-in. When that didn't lead to policy change, we scaled it up. Now we're doing boycotts.

Teens Take Charge did not pull punches. For example, a rally the group held at the NYCDOE central offices featured White youth wearing white tee-shirts and youth of color wearing black tee-shirts, under a banner that read, "De Blasio's School System."

Youth-led campaigns have played an increasingly important role in movements for educational justice over the past two decades.[3] Like other youth organizers, Teens Take Charge members drew heavily on their firsthand experiences of educational inequality to make a case for policy change. They collaborated with policy makers to develop new initiatives, and they applied public pressure when change came too slowly. However, most youth organizing campaigns are based in low-income, racially segregated neighborhoods and made up of overwhelmingly low-income youth of color.[4] Teens Take Charge was different, and noteworthy, because of its diverse membership base.

The year I spent with Teens Take Charge was a period of rapid change. Maimouna and other youth leaders told me that when they had first joined in the summer of 2018, there were "maybe five to ten" total

FIGURE 4.1. Teens Take Charge rally on the steps of NYCDOE headquarters at Tweed Courthouse, June 2019. (Photo by Dulce M. Marquez)

members at any given meeting. However, in the spring of 2019, Teens Take Charge members met with schools chancellor Richard Carranza, representatives from the mayor's office, and city council members on the sixty-fifth anniversary of *Brown v. Board of Education* to discuss segregation in New York City schools. Soon after, they held a press conference to publicize their plan to increase academic diversity, ban admissions screens, and direct additional resources to underenrolled high schools. Then, they organized a sit-in inside City Hall. Local media took note of these escalating actions. As Teens Take Charge's public presence grew, so did its membership. By the time I began observing the group in September 2019, most meetings were attended by more than forty members. Like Margot, I marveled at "the amount of teenagers who will come from all over the city to care about education, integration, and equity."

The group's rapid growth also increased its racial and socioeconomic diversity, which brought new challenges. Many scholars and advocates understand youth organizing as a tool to support, build coalitions among, and amplify the voices of racially and economically marginalized young people.[5] However, by the fall of 2019, a significant number of Teens Take Charge members identified as White and came from middle-class or professional families. Maimouna pointed out the trend in a leadership team meeting that fall: "as the organization gets stronger, the lighter it gets." Looking around the conference table, she gravely noted that Black and Latine members still outnumbered their White counterparts, but that might not be true for long. Other youth leaders agreed. Privately, Maimouna told me a month later, "I swear, it's like you blink, and it's all White."

In the initial TTC meetings during the spring of 2016, the only White people in the room were Taylor and one student. By September 2019, one-third of members in many Teens Take Charge meetings were White. The leadership team was made up of youth leaders (fourteen high school juniors and seniors, eight of whom identified as Black, four as White, and two as Latine), college advisers (four recent Teens Take Charge alums, three Latine and one Asian American), and Taylor.[6] With active support from college advisers and Taylor, youth leaders—about 35 percent of whom attended the city's most selective high schools—collaborated to develop organizational strategy, facilitate workshops, and lead members in public action, policy development, and communications work.

Civic Lessons: The Learning Environment of Youth Organizing

Youth leaders and Taylor saw Teens Take Charge's primary goal as policy change, rather than youth development. All the same, members did learn multiple, varied lessons from their work. This is not surprising: many scholars have found that youth organizing opens up new forms of learning that schools cannot offer.[7] Researchers have documented the multiple ways that organizing influences young people's civic engagement and personal growth.[8] As young activists engage in advocacy for educational equity, they critically examine the root causes of social problems, the wide range of possible policy responses, and the role of collective action in creating social change. Youth organizing groups offer what the curriculum scholar Carol D. Lee and her colleagues have described as a "robust learning environment" that supports emotional safety; allows participants to build on their prior knowledge; makes links to real-world challenges; encourages interrogation of sources of information, beliefs, and assumptions; provides opportunities to develop individual and collective efficacy; and ensures that participants wrestle with complex and contradictory ideas, including different perspectives within the group.[9]

The learning environment within Teens Take Charge made new identities, understandings, and actions available to members. Collectively, the group came to see students as more than consumers in a school marketplace and questioned the reasons why that segregated marketplace existed. They asked why Teens Take Charge was so diverse when their schools were not. They analyzed the roots of educational inequality and mastered the details of local policy making. They developed civic skills and knowledge outside the constraints of the formal educational system, with their peers, doing work that they valued. They did so in an integrated environment, collaborating across racial, socioeconomic, and academic boundaries toward their shared goal.

Choosing to Take Charge

One Monday afternoon in late September, I watched a youth leader facilitate a quick "check-in" by asking forty Teens Take Charge members to share a word or two about what brought them to that day's meeting. I jotted down their responses, which included,

> To fight
> True equity
> To change the future
> Integration and freedom
> Undeserved privilege
> For light
> To learn
> To connect
> To love
> To support
> To represent
> To push myself and listen
> For my people

Young people joined Teens Take Charge for a wide range of reasons: because their friends were there; because they had directly experienced the inequity of the city's school enrollment policies; because they wanted to get to know students who were different from themselves; because they were not finding answers to their urgent questions inside their schools. They cocreated a shared space in which they did more than describe systemic inequality; they took action. In Margot's words,

You know, it's like Mondays, I'll be so tired, and I'll be so frustrated and not even talking to people. And then I'll come and see . . . all these students coming for hours to just, like, fix the system. And they're all so supportive, and everyone just gets so excited. . . . It's like, that's what keeps me going, is going to our Monday meetings. And no matter how tired I am—I get home at like nine o'clock sometimes from those meetings, and then I have homework or whatever—it's just so inspiring to be with everyone.

Some Teens Take Charge members, like Margot, came to the group with a relatively abstract understanding of injustice. Others were inspired by more direct injuries. Amina, a Black member, lived in the Bronx and commuted ninety minutes each way to her highly selective high school in Manhattan. When we spoke the summer before her junior year, Amina had distinctly mixed feelings about her school. On the one hand, she had worked *really* hard in middle school. She was proud to have been admitted to a high school with a reputation for academic excellence. But when she arrived, she realized that she was one of the only Black students in her grade: "I was really excited to get in, and then I feel like after I got in, it's just like [in a disappointed tone] 'Wow.'" Amina remained grateful for all her school offered: multiple advanced placement (AP) courses, a rich array of clubs, laptop carts in every classroom. At the same time, her neighborhood, elementary school, and middle school had accustomed Amina to being "around Black and Brown people," and she grappled with the reality that "it's just hard not being around people that you're like."

Amina worked hard to make friends in her new school. She knew that her mostly White classmates, who had also attended segregated schools, had limited experience developing friendships across racial boundaries. But a series of events made Amina wonder whether she should stop trying. During an advisory class at the end of her ninth-grade year, a White classmate whom Amina considered a friend handed her a piece of paper wrapped around a tampon. Amina unscrolled the note and saw a message with the N-word that said that Black people have no rights, using the hashtags #truth and #monkey. Talking about this experience a few years later, Amina reminded me that this message was delivered in her advisory class, which is designed to welcome ninth graders to the school, encourage them to think about others' perspectives, and promote diversity and inclusion.

Amina told me that when she returned to school the next fall, several students of color had transferred out due to stress caused by racial tensions in the school. The following spring, soon after her school had switched to remote instruction due to COVID-19 lockdowns, someone "Zoom bombed" an online class and called Amina the N-word in the class chat. Her principal called Amina to say how sorry he was that she had (twice now) been exposed to these attacks and explained that the school would soon offer an official response. Amina waited and waited, but that was it. Nothing more was said or done. When I talked with her a few months after that incident, Amina sighed and told me, "I don't get excitement from being in school. I just try to do what I can." Looking back on the experience a few years later, Amina realized that there was no way the school could have identified the Zoom bomber. But at the time, she interpreted her principal's inaction as indifference.

When Amina and I spoke that summer before her senior year of high school, she had set herself two main goals. The first was personal: she would make the most of every opportunity to get into a good college. But Amina also set a second, political goal because she felt a responsibility to do more than just "act like a normal student." Her goal for the remainder of high school was to shift her school's racial culture. Amina intimately understood why Black and Brown students were so uncomfortable that they left her selective high school; she wanted to change school norms, "so that more freshmen [of color] don't have to leave." Addressing the school's racial climate would also increase the school's diversity, which Amina believed would benefit all students. However, she was not initially sure how to reach this goal.

A few months earlier, New York City had locked down due to the COVID pandemic. Now that Amina did not have a long subway ride to and from school, she had much more free time. She researched online, found Teens Take Charge, and began attending Zoom meetings. The conversations at Teens Take Charge helped Amina better understand her educational trajectory. She had always known that her schools were racially stratified: she attended elementary and middle school with Black and Latine students in the Bronx and high school with White and Asian students in Manhattan. But before she joined Teens Take Charge, Amina "didn't realize *how* segregated New York City schools were." Previously, she explained, "I was just like, 'Oh, okay, that's normal.'" As she talked with other Teens Take Charge members, Amina began to view her school's laptop carts and AP courses differently. She compared her experiences at selective high schools with those of her friends who attended schools in her own neighborhood—schools that had far fewer resources than hers but also where her friends felt far less socially isolated. Rather than feeling lucky or unlucky to have left, she felt "kind of mad. . . . There was no reason" why she should have to go so far from home to access educational resources.

Reflecting on the three hours of travel each day between her segregated, mostly Black and Brown neighborhood and her segregated, mostly White and Asian American school, Amina had a new lens onto educational inequality. Now she understood how school zone lines worked and the ways they overlapped with neighborhood income. That correlation did not "seem like a coincidence." She quickly came to feel that her principal's apparent indifference to racist incidents was also not a coincidence. Amina's new understanding of the policies underlying her experiences clarified her dual purpose: to get what she personally needed out of an inequitable system and to challenge the racist status quo for other students of color at her school.

When students finally returned to New York City high schools the following year, Amina sat down with her principal to share her experience, saying, "This is what I've gone through at your school. Make sure no other Black student has to do this again." Amina spent the next year of the pandemic working to change admissions policies at her high school, in collaboration with her principal and with coaching from the

Teens Take Charge leadership team. She told me the struggle to "fight a fifty-year school segregation war in New York City while people were dying from a disease" consumed all her time that year but also was powerful motivation to keep fighting.

Many other members also came to Teens Take Charge out of a dual sense of exhaustion and purpose. Maimouna told me that she joined Teens Take Charge because one day in class, she found herself "trying to convince" her classmates that they "*do* have power." Upset and unsure how to find other young people who saw themselves as powerful, Maimouna, like Amina, "started going to Google and just do whatever a teenager does, look up organizations for teens who want to make a change." She found Teens Take Charge. After attending one meeting, Maimouna was hooked: "Being able to be in a room where I can see students who have so much confidence, so much radiance, so much power, who believe so firmly in the things that they're saying, who are unapologetically just honest, was just amazing to me. And then, they started talking about segregation. I was like, 'Oh, I don't know what I've gotten myself into, but I want to feel the same type of power that they feel when they talk to me.'" Members like Amina and Maimouna came to Teens Take Charge in search of ways to make change; they found not only a shared sense of possibility but also an opportunity to learn collectively.

Creating a "Mini-School": Peer Teaching and Learning in Teens Take Charge

Like many young people, Maimouna had long noticed the gaps between what she was taught in her US history and government classes and her own lived experiences—a disjuncture that is often particularly acute for young people of color in segregated schools.[10] Teens Take Charge offered Maimouna a chance to learn the "true history," to situate her experience in broader social structures. After joining Teens Take Charge, Maimouna recognized that the Black students in her high school were "sitting in classes" where they were "being taught about Europe": "We rarely talk about Africa. We rarely talk about Latin America." Maimouna concluded that students are "being taught from a curriculum that teaches" students that they "have nothing to contribute": "And so, TTC made me realize that the way that we perceive ourselves in the world is very important if we want to talk about going on to create anything."

Soon after that realization, Maimouna started "to read books from people like W. E. B. Du Bois, from people like Martin Luther King, people like Malcolm X, and learning about just like what America truly did, how step after step after step, at every chance of freedom or liberation or success, there was a foot getting ready to stomp on them." Her new understanding of Black history profoundly influenced Maimouna's analysis of not only United States society but also herself: "[It] really gave me a sense of who I am and made it my identity, which makes it easier for me to walk around in any space and feel solid in who I am." Maimouna believed this learning could be liberatory for other Teens Take Charge members. Immediately before the COVID-19 pandemic, she proposed starting a "mini-school" so that, together, members could learn the history that "their school does not give them." She saw this project as more than an opportunity for Teens Take Charge to "fill in the gaps"—it would be a way for young people to stop "demanding and begging" that policy makers and educators do things differently and instead create "the very thing" that they were looking for by themselves, for themselves.

Although Maimouna's ambitious vision was never realized, Teens Take Charge already operated, in many ways, as a mini-school. Youth leaders collaborated with Taylor to develop curricula that taught members civic knowledge, such as the history of school segregation in New York City, the structures of local government, and community organizing strategies. Members were shocked to realize that their US history courses had taught them nothing about the 1964 school boycotts involving half a million New York City students and teachers, one of the largest protests of the civil rights movement. They read a selection about the boycott from Jeanne Theoharris's book *A More Beautiful and Terrible History*; Theoharris came to a meeting to answer their questions about the role that young people could play in the long struggle for school integration. Other workshops drew on a wide range of materials, from archival newspaper clippings to community organizing manuals. Together, members identified central actors in and key components of the city's education policy system. The leadership team viewed this teaching and learning as essential. One evening, Maimouna reminded the general meeting how important it was to know what they were talking about: "if you're fighting for a cause you don't understand, you're going to make a fool out of us."

Members told me that they engaged in far more depth in their reading and research for Teens Take Charge than they did even for their favorite classes at school, simply because they knew they would *use* what they had learned. As Maimouna explained, "There used to be moments in the beginning where I would go into a Town Hall, and somebody would ask me a question, and I would pause, because I did not know how to answer it. And so, that made me want to research more into all of these issues." At times, members took their research far beyond the bounds of the group's meetings. Multiple TTC members studied school segregation policies for independent research papers or "capstone" courses; they treated their new knowledge as ammunition, marshaling evidence to counter teachers who questioned their analyses. Others pored over demographic data from their own schools, confronting their school administration about "problematic" admissions and discipline policies.

The similarity between elements of Teens Take Charge and formal social studies instruction was undeniable. At times, members were assigned readings as weekly "homework." One evening I watched a youth leader announce to the meeting, "I'm going to cold-call," just as a teacher might. In a small group discussion, I observed as members discussed newspaper coverage of the 1964 school boycott, making connections to recent reporting on Teens Take Charge actions, backtracking to clarify the distinction between de facto and de jure segregation, tracing the retreat from desegregation court orders since the early 1980s, and making connections between these events and contemporary school choice policies. The ease with which members referenced facts, discussed shared

FIGURE 4.2. Detail from Teens Take Charge press conference marking the sixty-fifth anniversary of *Brown v. Board of Education*, May 2019. (Photo by Dulce M. Marquez)

texts, and analyzed relationships between policy, history, and politics made my former-history-teacher self want to cry happy tears—not simply because members demonstrated nuanced understanding of complex historical concepts but because they were so sure that understanding mattered. I often found myself reflecting on a member's testimony that Teens Take Charge was "what every classroom should look like."

Teens Take Charge prompted some members to undertake projects that extended their academic skills, even as they used what they learned to challenge school and city policy. At the same time, it may have left members without similar dispositions—or the skills or time required to independently embark on this work—more in the margins. What if people did not want to do additional reading outside of school? What if they found policy texts challenging to unpack? What if they were busy after school, working part-time jobs or caring for family members? I sometimes overheard members whispering to each other about not having done the reading, much as they might in a high school classroom. In such moments, the Teens Take Charge learning environment appeared less than liberatory.

One alternative to "homework assignments" was to engage in the "Civil Discourse" WhatsApp group. Youth leaders had worried that frequent late-night texts about current events—while important—might overshadow logistical announcements in the Teens Take Charge group chat. Not willing to sacrifice either conversation, they created a "Civil Discourse" chat group, in which members went back and forth about definitions of racism, tensions between Black and Asian American students in New York City schools, and the various roles that schools could play in creating social change. Youth leaders—many of whom were perceived by peers as experts on education policy—took a backseat in this forum. This alternative space offered other members, who often identified as less "academic" and tended to be relatively quiet during Teens Take Charge meetings, an opportunity to lead the conversation. However, while many considered such "civil discourse" exciting and generative, it did not play a significant role in the group's central work: advocating for new high school admissions policies.

From Policy Targets to Policy Actors

Monika, a Latina youth leader, sat down with me one afternoon to describe how Teens Take Charge had changed her thinking about New York City schools. She said that before she joined Teens Take Charge, she knew "there was a problem": "I knew I wasn't receiving the same level of educational opportunities as other students were." People like her family and the staff at her after-school academic support program had consistently communicated their belief that Monika could and would overcome these challenges. But after she joined Teens Take Charge, she saw the situation differently. She learned, "Okay, this is why the problem exists. This is how it happened. And this is what you can do outside of, like, trying to play catch-up: try and prevent it from happening to other students." As she shifted her focus from her own individual experience to the collective impact of school segregation, Monika also moved from thinking about how policy affected her to how she could affect policy.

Teens Take Charge encouraged members to think like organizers, not students. In Margot's words, "I've been in the school system my entire life," but Teens Take Charge helped her understand the NYCDOE as a political system. Members came to these new understandings by engaging in the "practices of critique and collective agency" that the learning scientist Ben Kirshner explains are central to both civic learning and youth organizing.[11] Kaden, a Black youth leader, described how his views shifted as a result of considering and reconsidering how policy is made: "Before I joined Teens Take Charge, when I thought of 'government,' I just thought of a whole bunch of people in suits. That's what pops up into my mind sometimes. Now I see, I really get to see the breakdown from, like, the city council and our senators and the mayor and the governor. So, I see there's different levels and that power is allocated to people differently." Kaden and other members were not all that impressed by what they observed. They described local Community Education Council and Department of Education meetings as "disheartening" and "eye-opening." Monika concluded that local elected officials are "bullshitters" who "don't really do anything that they say they're gonna do." From Teens Take Charge, she learned that "it takes mobilization of people to actually create change": "We can't—you can't—rely on systems to do it for you or bureaucracy to do it for you." Monika and Teens Take Charge members learned that the only way to make the system more equal was to "organize from the ground up."

Teens Take Charge based its work in two fundamental principles: young people have the power to change public policy, and they must do so together. When members became overwhelmed by the enormity of their goals, youth leaders reminded them of the central roles they could and did play in the city's policy system. At a planning meeting for a protest, for example, members were afraid they would not be able to pull off the public action. They worried that other students would not join them, that they would be too small a group to make an impact. Kelvin, a Latine youth leader, looked around the circle and assured them, "You *have* the tools. You are experts in your schools." They could leverage that expertise to reach their goals.

FIGURE 4.3. Detail from Teens Take Charge school strike at Brooklyn Borough Hall, January 2020. (Photo by Dulce M. Marquez)

In contrast to neoliberal policies and policy discourses that foreground students' individual choices, members approached their political work as a collective practice. In that same meeting, eight Teens Take Charge members worked with the leadership team to plan their "school strike," a walkout to protest segregation. Three of these organizers were White girls from a highly selective high school on the top two floors of a NYCDOE building; five were Black and Latino boys from the technical school colocated below. A month before the event, they were figuring out logistics and public speaking responsibilities. When one of the organizers from the technical school said he would rather not give a speech, Anthony—a Black youth leader who, like these students, attended an unscreened school with a poor reputation—shook his head, smiling, and said, "We're going to talk this week. We're going to make you a star." When a White organizer from the selective high school reported difficulties getting buy-in from her school's Black Student Union, Kelvin suggested getting support from the organizers in the school downstairs. Together, the team brainstormed recruitment strategies and role-played approaching potential allies, with Kelvin urging the members to "believe in the work" and "embody the change" they want to see at their schools. In interactions like these, youth leaders focused on the group's shared goals, while offering support to emerging leaders—many of whom lacked the confidence of their peers attending selective high schools.

That school strike, the first in a series of seven walkouts across the city that year, was a success. Over 150 students walked out into a public park near their school, holding a "Strike for Integration" banner and chanting, "Integrate *now*." In the park, the chants continued: "Education is a right, not just for the rich and White!" and "Chancellor Carranza, our voices matter!" A Black boy from the technical school spoke through a bullhorn that amplified his story of being "so jealous of the resources" that he saw in the school upstairs. He explained that now he recognized that he had been "blaming the wrong people"; he needed to "direct his anger to de Blasio and the DOE." A White girl with pink hair described experiences in her own segregated, well-resourced public school. An organizer from the technical school closed out the speeches, assuring the crowd that while this was just one Monday, it would be "a catalyst for Tuesday" and that they would continue their advocacy on behalf of their "little brothers and sisters." Cameras everywhere captured the series of events for Instagram, Twitter, and local news outlets; reporters pulled aside organizers to ask about their plans for integration. Then the school strike was over. The group divided to reenter the school building: a line of mostly White and Asian American students at the entrance to the selective high school upstairs, a longer line of mostly Black and Latine students returning to the technical school downstairs.

Teens Take Charge members refused to play the role of "policy targets," constrained by the system that was supposed to serve them.[12] They came to see themselves as actors capable of shifting the policies that shaped their experiences in schools. Margot explained that she continued to do this work, despite her frequent exhaustion, because Teens Take

Charge was different from other places, where people "talk and talk" but "nothing ever gets done." Like other members, she believed that despite substantial obstacles, they were "actually making changes": "Maybe all our policies haven't been enacted, but we have changed the conversations. We have gained power for the students." At their schools, through public testimony, and within Teens Take Charge meetings, members narrated, monitored, translated, critiqued, and resisted the rules and processes that targeted them.[13] They did not want students to exercise a token "voice" within an inequitable policy system. They wanted to make the system itself more equitable.

Teens Take Charge resisted attempts to position young people as future adults, future citizens, or even future activists. Like the youth organizers that Kwon studied, they developed a shared student activist identity that was "strategic, issue-based, and informed by political equality."[14] They knew that they mattered right now: their collective stories and actions could change education policy.

"I Always Felt Critical" and "I Had No Idea": Separate Starting Points in a Segregated System

I think, you know, growing up in a public school system—especially if you don't have anything to compare it to: I've never gone to private schools; I've never gone to very elite public schools—so I've always kind of accepted it as the norm. This is how it is. This is exactly how it's supposed to be. I've gone to elementary, middle, and high school in very under-resourced public schools, but maybe that's just what it is. Maybe that's just—that's just how I accepted it to be. But when you join an organization that's actively fighting against that and they're making sure that students like me aren't thinking that their horrible experience is the norm, that's when you really know that it has made an impact.
—Adara, Asian American, junior

Given the intense segregation of the New York City public school system, all Teens Take Charge members brought considerable firsthand knowledge of segregated schools to their work. However, like Adara, many members had at some point normalized the effects of this segregation—they thought that their resource-scarce public schools were "exactly how it's supposed to be." In both informal conversations and structured workshops, Teens Take Charge members relentlessly and repeatedly reminded each other that school segregation in New York City was neither accidental nor incidental. Members frequently reviewed a long list of NYCDOE policy decisions that contributed to notoriously inequitable school and student outcomes. The youth leader Kelvin told me that this understanding was foundational: "Like, you're not talking about, 'There's no Black and Brown kids in this school.' It's like *no*. [pauses for emphasis] They're *segregated*. . . . And you realize, a lot of the issues that could have been fixed with that were not."

Teens Take Charge offered members an opportunity to situate their personal school and neighborhood experiences in broader patterns of structural inequality. However, because these lived experiences varied widely, so did members' responses to what they learned. Members who attended majority Black and Latine schools serving low-income communities had very different perspectives than those who attended the city's selective high schools, which were disproportionately White and Asian American. They came in with different questions about their experiences and took away overlapping, yet distinct, answers. These distinctions influenced not only members' individual learning but also the group's capacity to meet its goals.

When I asked Sienna, a Black student who attended a selective high school, if Teens Take Charge had changed how she thought about her well-resourced, majority-White school, she replied with a wry smile, "Well, it hasn't made me like it any more." After we both chuckled, Sienna continued, "It's not so much that it changed the way that I feel about my high school, but I think it made it easier for me to put my feelings into actual words, because there was always something that felt off to me. . . . I feel like I always felt critical of my school, but Teens Take Charge kind of helped me understand *why* I felt critical." She had "always felt sort of out of place" in her school, but she experienced Teens Take Charge as an opportunity to "click turn," to pivot and "make connections between things that have happened however many years ago and things that are still happening" at her school.

Natalie had also long been aware of structural inequality. Unlike Sienna and Teens Take Charge members who attended selective schools, Natalie was intimately familiar with what it meant for a school to fail its students. Still, she told me that she deeply valued the opportunity to better understand how and why her community lacked resources: "Like, I didn't know anything about redlining or how when groups of African American people came from the South, they settled in certain parts of New York City and, because of segregation, they were never allowed to move. Like, that just never clicked to me. So that—that's one example. But also just, as I continue every day to learn more about the history of systemic racism in this country, it allows me to make connections to my daily life." Natalie told me that Teens Take Charge helps her "make sense of everything that's happened." Her analysis had become structural: "Now I know that my school is the way that it is not necessarily because of, like, the teachers or the staff or the students. It's just because this system was designed to make things work like that." Teens Take Charge was the place where "it first clicked" in her head "that it's not a coincidence."

That both Natalie and Amina used the word "coincidence" as they described their emerging policy analyses was not, well, a coincidence. Teens Take Charge taught students of color to view their educational trajectories as the result of systemic, rather than individual, failures. This understanding fueled their personal and political commitment to policy change. Many Black and Latine members like Natalie described their work as part of an effort to improve the chances of their younger siblings and cousins, even though it was too late to change their own high school placements.

However, the fact remained that many Teens Take Charge members attended more selective high schools than their peers did. Members of color who attended these schools often struggled with the role they played in the city's unequal educational system. Mei, who identified as both Asian American and White, told me that at first, it was so hard to say, "Oh, we should unscreen schools," since "screened schools have always worked for me." Teens Take Charge offered Mei opportunities to revisit her own personal experiences, even as she examined and re-examined city policies and school attendance data. Mei explained, "It really became clear to me that, like, the system I was in was, like, created to benefit me. But that I was losing a lot from it and that it wasn't working for anybody." This recognition prompted Mei to reconsider not only her admission to a selective high school but also the way that "systems of White privilege" position Asian Americans as a "model minority group." Mei explained that she wanted Teens Take Charge members and other integration advocates "to think really critically before grouping, like, wealthy white kids [she] grew up with, with the very poor Asian kids [she] went to cram school with." Teens Take Charge did not increase Mei's or Natalie's awareness of injustice. These young people of color were already acutely aware of the problems; that is why they joined the fight for school integration. What Teens Take Charge offered was a framework members could use to make sense of and respond to structural inequality.

White Teens Take Charge members tended to follow a different trajectory. Like members of color, these young people made connections between their own experiences and citywide policies, between historical and contemporary inequality, and between what they learned and the actions they took. And like members of color, White members critically analyzed connections, gaps, and tensions within these patterns. But whereas Black and Latine members sought new explanations for racial inequality, White members came to recognize the extent of this inequality, often for the first time. Indeed, many White members had stories about how they "found out" about school and neighborhood segregation. Paula, for example, was slightly embarrassed as she told me that before she came to a Teens Take Charge meeting, she "had absolutely no idea": "Like, I'm gonna be so honest. I did not know how segregated the system was.... Learning about that is just very, very eye-opening." Paula was surprised by what she learned about structural inequality at Teens Take Charge—rather than explaining something that had long angered her, this view of segregation "changed how [she] thought about [her] school." Similarly, Zoë, another White member who attended a well-resourced, highly selective high school, told me that it took time for her to reconcile her knowledge of the unequal school system with "the complex ways that [her] own school is a part of the problem." Looking back, she told me that when she learned about school segregation, she "was like, 'Holy shit. My life has been a little bit of a lie.'" This sense of shock propelled Zoë, Paula, and other White members to action.

"Maybe It's Just a Black and Brown People Thing": Diverging Lessons in an Integrated Space

An "Open-Minded" Community

In some ways, Teens Take Charge appeared to be an exemplary integrated community, dedicated to bridging racial and social boundaries. Monika, a Latine youth leader, called the space truly "open-minded" and "the first outside-of-school community" that she had "ever really had." She chuckled as she told me that in most spaces, if you talked to someone you did not know, they would "just look at you like"—and here, Monika grimaced, making a face that somehow appeared simultaneously snobby and confused—but that was not at all the case at Teens Take Charge: "That's exactly the point, is to get to know other students you've never seen before, probably would've never seen before if you didn't come here. And, like, you just talk to them about literally anything political, and they're automatically like, 'Okay, well, we're gonna have this conversation right now.'" Lina, a Black member, emphatically agreed. She told me that even though people "had different viewpoints on a lot of things" and "would debate on everything," "each and every one of us in that room wanted to see change." That "drive for change" brought members together, allowing them to see new points of view and offering multiple chances to develop the skills and perspectives valued by advocates of diverse schools.[15] Many diversity advocates have considered Teens Take Charge their proof of concept: a racially and socioeconomically integrated community, devoted to shared learning and collective action. However, White members and Black and Latine members learned very different lessons from this integrated space.

"The Place We're Actually Going to Experience Diversity"

Many White members saw Teens Take Charge as a rare opportunity to get outside their segregated schools and neighborhoods. Margot, who was enrolled in a highly selective, disproportionately White high school, explained that Teens Take Charge was "the most diverse, actually representative of the city, space" she had ever been in": "It's like, well, if our classrooms aren't going to be diverse, well, this is the place we're actually going to experience diversity." Ramona, like other White members I interviewed, told me that she joined Teens Take Charge in part because the environment was "much more racially diverse than a lot of other environments" she had been in: "And I wanted that." She first attended a meeting when a youth leader reached out to her, looking for students from her selective high school to organize a school strike. Prior to that meeting, Ramona "hadn't thought that much" about school segregation, nor had she ever talked with the Black and Latine students who attended the other school located in her building. Teens Take Charge offered Ramona a way into these conversations. Ramona learned, "[They had] lines out of their guidance counselor's door for college information when, like, not only do I have a separate college and guidance counselor at my school, but both are very accessible. And I feel very lucky to be able to and have taken advantage of both." What she learned made Ramona see her own school experiences differently: "I just can't imagine having it another way, sort of, so it was really eye-opening for me to hear other people's frustrations."

Like other White members, Ramona tried to "really think" about when to speak and when to remain silent in Teens Take Charge. When I asked her why this was so important, she got stuck. Ramona's speech faltered uncharacteristically as she struggled to explain her reasoning: "Because I've only gone to majority-White and wealthy schools. It's like I do have a lot to say, and it's not about not having enough to say, but I think it's like, um, me just talking about those experiences. And, like, 'everyone should have this' isn't enough. . . . My voice isn't as important, sort of, just because I'm not the one that is hurt as much with the—like, yeah, obviously everyone is suffering, but I'm not the one." Ramona's determination "not to dominate" and to make "sure other people's voices get heard" was shared by many White Teens Take Charge members. Much of the group's work was public-facing, and people had to take turns for opportunities like speaking to reporters, sharing testimony, or leading rallies. I often saw White members deliberately stepping out of the spotlight and taking on work that was more behind the scenes. They were learning to decenter their own voices and experiences.

Ramona's approach resembled that of many White members who saw Teens Take Charge as a way "to hear more about different people's experiences." Doing so made it possible for her to learn more about the social and policy worlds surrounding her, while pushing her individual growth. These young White people reaped the benefits of diversity: they learned about others' experiences in a segregated system and, in the process, often developed new insights about their own. As a result, most White members saw the group's diversity as an unalloyed good.

Unfortunately, the benefits of what some integration researchers call "exposure" to racial diversity appeared to be unevenly distributed among Teens Take Charge members. While many members of color also noted the value of "hearing somebody else's story," they rarely emphasized the role that racial diversity played in making them more "open-minded." And while White students repeatedly and emphatically told me that they loved learning and working in a racially diverse environment, Black and Latine members often expressed ambivalence.

Maimouna, for example, acknowledged that diversity could be beneficial for students in a segregated school system that did not give them the chance to hang out with people of different races "on the regular." And yet she was not sure that she herself benefited from this opportunity. Maimouna loved her own "historically Black high school" and did not see it as a problem that "in all of [her] experience in the school system," she had "only had at most a handful of white kids in [her] class." She knew many people in Teens Take Charge would say, "That is bad. You know, this is why we always talk about integration." But Maimouna was not so sure: "I felt represented at my school, not just by students but also for the teachers and the principal and the fact that they could understand where I'm coming from. The fact that when they look at me, they see greatness, and they don't see a future criminal." Her school community helped Maimouna believe, as a young Black woman, "I can do what I need to do," and that in turn made her "more motivated to learn."

Conversations at Teens Take Charge convinced Maimouna that her experience was far outside the norm for most Black students in segregated schools; she listened carefully to other members' accounts of racist teachers and scarce resources. She knew that access to more selective high schools played an important part in educational opportunity. However, she also knew that Black students in those selective high schools were not likely to have teachers and administrators who understood their experiences. She believed that Black spaces could play an important part in the education of students like herself. However, Teens Take Charge was emphatically not that kind of space. As Maimouna had repeatedly warned the leadership team, as the group integrated, it was becoming more and more White.

"I Don't Fit In": Wrestling with White Norms

Monika, the Latine youth leader who so deeply valued crossing social boundaries, realized that the recent increase in White membership had made it more difficult to recruit new Black and Latine members: "They come here, and they see that it's, like—there's a lot of White students. And if there aren't White students, there are a lot of students that look like them that don't go to schools that they go to. So it's like, 'Okay, um, I don't fit in. I don't really want to be here.'" The feeling of not fitting in was exacerbated by the group's physical environment. Because Teach for America offered Teens Take Charge free office space, members met on the twelfth floor of a skyscraper on Wall Street. Before going upstairs, young people had to line up in the gold-leaf-encrusted lobby, waiting for a security guard to check their identification. Monika told me that a lot of new members "were like, whoa, like this is Wall Street, . . . and it's like they don't recognize that they do belong here, whether they have been here before or not." This feeling of not belonging was not only a recruitment obstacle but also a fundamental challenge to the group's work.

Even as Teens Take Charge members devoted enormous time and effort to integrating the city's high schools, they struggled with racialized norms within the group. Lina, the Black member who shared Monika's appreciation for the group's diversity, told me that when she first came to a Teens Take Charge meeting, she felt that it was "very, very different" and thought, "that is not my setting at all." Regina, a Black youth leader, reported that she knew quite a few members who felt they had to adapt their interactional styles in meetings, even though she herself did not. She shrugged it off: "Maybe it's just a Black and Brown people thing is, we just have to keep assimilating to different places and different situations."

Other youth leaders were not as resigned. In one small group discussion, Natalie, who was Latine, argued that the group was "too prim and proper" for many students like herself; she hesitated to invite friends from her unscreened high school because she did not want them "to come in here and automatically have to codeswitch." Kelvin told me that while there were many Black and Latine youth leaders, most of them attended "certain schools in the city that have more resources": "And there's a type of, I think, character that you have in those schools." Kelvin believed that many youth leaders had learned to "assimilate" at school, where they were taught not to use "the vernacular [they] use at home." He believed youth leaders brought those lessons with them to Teens Take Charge, which set the tone for other members, who often did not recognize that their work would be stronger if it came from "their genuine self." Kelvin hesitated a bit, trying to explain why this mattered, then went on, "Like, when you're a successful person, that usually means you meet the standards of, like—to me, it's whiteness."

Over the course of the 2019–20 program year, Teens Take Charge members wrestled with the role that whiteness played in their integrated learning environment. Maimouna and other Black and Latine youth leaders repeatedly expressed concerns that many new members did "not feel the connection to the problem" that a lot of them felt. Whenever they issued these warnings, heads around the room nodded. The leadership team held a series of discussions about ways the space was not welcoming for students of color and students who did not attend selective schools. In an uncomfortable conversation at a general meeting, one Black member argued that Teens Take Charge "started off as a refuge, and now it's something people need to seek refuge from, because they leave who they are at the door." Many Black and Latine youth leaders pushed back. Monika urged the room to remember that members "are the people in charge of the space" and if there are problems, they "have to fix the situation" themselves. However, the leadership team seemed unsure how to take on this work amid their pressing responsibilities of planning public actions and advocating for new policies.

These tensions strained the relationships and collective labor that were central to the group's success. Youth organizing can be exhausting under any circumstance, and the conditions facing Teens Take Charge were particularly intense: extremely rapid growth, heightened public scrutiny, and increasingly ambitious campaign goals. These were high school students who had to deal with the competing demands of family responsibilities, classwork, college applications, and jobs. In a meeting late one evening, the leadership team nodded empathetically as one youth leader said she wanted to go home and cry in the shower.

As the only adult staff member available to provide support, Taylor was stretched extremely thin; what is more, he was a White man whose primary goal was to change educational policy, rather than support young people's development. It is not surprising that the group and its members struggled under these conditions.

During the time that I observed, four out of eight Black youth leaders—including Maimouna and Regina—left the organization. Others expressed renewed determination to challenge the group's dynamics. But by March 2020, New York was the epicenter of the COVID pandemic. As Teens Take Charge rapidly adjusted to Zoom meetings and Instagram organizing, the group's internal norms and focus shifted quite dramatically. It is difficult to know what might have happened if things had proceeded as "normal"; it is also possible that the pandemic played a role in the departure of several Black youth leaders. By December 2021, Teens Take Charge had paused all organizing activities in order to reflect on its internal culture and set new goals.

The Hidden Curriculum of Integration Organizing

At Teens Take Charge, members learned that they were the subjects, not the objects, of educational policy. They refused to be treated as consumers making a choice among the city's high schools, positioning themselves as citizens who had the collective power to push back against a segregated system. What is more, they asserted that power *right now*. These young people demanded to be understood by local policy makers not as future voters or citizens-in-the-making but as integral parts of a complex policy landscape. The sheer volume of news coverage related to their demonstrations, town halls, and organizing campaigns was evidence of their collective capacity to shape policy discourse. Between 2018 and 2020, the group's work was featured in the *New York Times* and the subject of several short documentaries for *Teen Vogue*; their protests were covered by more than fifty articles and news segments in both local and national media. The impact of their campaigns on educational policy was less clear (in part due to the wrenching changes to New York City schools resulting from the COVID-19 pandemic), but members were proud to claim several victories in battles for funding youth programs and shifting public views of segregation in New York City schools.

Organizing offered these young people opportunities to push back against not only the enrollment and choice policies that contributed to school segregation but also the values and relationships that these neoliberal policies and policy discourses promoted. Their actions echoed those of English teachers studied by Stephen J. Ball and his colleagues, Chicago students navigating the high school choice process followed by Kate Phillippo, and Philadelphia teen activists observed by Sonia Rosen.[16] Like these policy actors, Teens Take Charge members developed identities distinct from their understandings of themselves as students (individuals who are expected to comply with the educational system) or even stakeholders (individuals who are invested in the outcomes of policy decisions but do not shape the process).

Members' deep learning in this informal environment illuminates the degree to which the norms and assumptions of our educational system limit what students learn. In some ways, members' experiences in Teens Take Charge resembled the demands of high school: they were introduced to unfamiliar ideas and information; they undertook challenging tasks; and they acquired new analytic and communication skills. However, Teens Take Charge members acquired knowledge in service of deeply held personal and political goals; they assigned *themselves* authentic, high-stakes tasks, rather than completing graded assignments; and they learned in relationship with their peers, in a context that was dramatically more diverse than any classroom they had encountered. As a result, these young people developed complex understandings of what we often call "social studies": history, civics, and government.

However, going beyond the bounds of the formal educational system does not make everything possible. Like public schools, community-based organizations also have hidden curricula. While Teens Take

Charge members learned very different lessons in their shared, integrated space than they did in their segregated high schools, these lessons were still racialized. Young people came to the group with vastly different experiences of racism; their diverging understandings of power and public policy built on those varied foundations. Reckoning with the hidden curriculum of this youth organizing is, in Kwon's words, "not to argue against that organizing or against political activism. It is to seriously recognize how such projects are embedded in multiple axes of power."[17]

On the one hand, Teens Take Charge showed members that segregation was not and never could be "normal." As Monika explained, the first thing she said when recruiting new members was, "You won't understand how important the issue is and how real the issue is until you come to one of the meetings": "'Cause even when I was doing the research, there are all these numbers and statistics and stuff, but it doesn't, like, really make sense to you or matter as much to you until you go to these meetings and listen to the people who are having experiences that you never have even thought of." Teens Take Charge required members to learn alongside people very different from themselves, and both White members and members of color valued that opportunity.

As a result of White Teens Take Charge members' integrated organizing for school integration, they learned lessons that many other White kids never absorbed; they came to criticize what Maggie Hagerman has called the "many unearned advantages they receive in their day-to-day lives."[18] This critique fueled their dedication to the organization's work, but it also had its limits. I asked several White members who attended well-resourced selective high schools if they would make different school choices, now that they had learned about segregation in New York City schools. Several said they would. Others would not. While they all learned to appreciate diversity, only some White members were ready to renounce the school resources derived from a segregated system.

Black and Latine members learned very different lessons. Like their White peers, members of color came to recognize their power as young people. At the same time, some members questioned the extent to which their group was truly integrated. Almost all Teens Take Charge members developed cultural flexibility, but only Black and Latine members were asked to "leave who they are at the door" in order to do so. When I spoke with alumni several years later, most told me that they deeply valued the advocacy skills, the nuanced understanding of public policy, and the relationships that they developed through Teens Take Charge. They reported reflecting often on these lessons as they navigated predominantly White institutions or worked in other social movements. However, others felt marginalized by Teens Take Charge, an experience they found particularly disturbing given the group's goals.

Teens Take Charge alumni were deeply divided on how to make sense of these tensions. As Mei looked back on her experiences several years later, she told me, "I think that TTC was trying to reimagine the way we interacted with one another. It wasn't just about creating equality and racial integration. It was really, like, how you create a school where people are able to live in a diverse, a *truly* diverse environment. . . . The idea wasn't that it was conflict-free but that there was power in that diversity and in the things that come out of it." Looking back, some members felt strongly that any racial harm situated within Teens Take Charge revealed fundamental flaws in this approach. Others disagreed, focusing on Teens Take Charge's contributions to educational justice: the shifts in public conversations about school segregation, opportunities for young people to participate in policy deliberations, and avenues for individual growth and learning. As an observer, I came to the unsatisfying conclusion that none of us was sure how to reckon with the trade-offs inherent in the group's risky and ambitious endeavor. As Du Bois argues, diversity is far from magical. Integration can yield positive results, but it can also pain both individuals and organizations. And it is almost certain to be messy.

Conclusion

Several years have passed since the events this book describes. Hazel and Marquise have moved on from P.S. 411 to middle school; Michelle is finishing up high school; Teens Take Charge members have graduated the public school system altogether. The city's policy ecosystem has also experienced major changes. In 2018, Mayor de Blasio replaced schools chancellor Carmen Fariña with Richard Carranza. Under Chancellor Carranza, the New York City Department of Education started talking about school integration, as well as diversity. However, very few school enrollment policies actually changed. This maintenance of the status quo was in part due to de Blasio and Carranza's focus on state-mandated admissions policies at the city's eight highly selective specialized high schools. The resulting controversy dominated conversations about New York City school segregation for almost a year, sidelining discussions of admissions policies at the eighteen hundred elementary, middle, and high schools that are directly under NYCDOE control.

In 2020, advocacy for school integration was largely overshadowed by debates over whether and how to reopen school buildings during the COVID-19 pandemic. Amid this unprecedented terrain, Chancellor Carranza pushed for changes to school enrollment policies, arguing that it would be a shame to "waste a good crisis" that offered "an opportunity to finally push and move and be very strategic in a very aggressive way" for an "equity agenda."[1] The NYCDOE changed admissions policies for elementary school gifted and talented programs and selective middle schools that fall. Controversy over the timing, framing, and substance of these policy changes contributed to Carranza's resignation in early 2021, several months before the Democratic mayoral primary that nominated de Blasio's successor.

In part due to controversy over schooling during COVID-19, that primary race was crowded with candidates hotly debating education policy. Teens Take Charge held a widely watched mayoral candidate forum on Zoom that many observers called the best of the season. Members facilitated the conversation, asking candidates to explain their stances on youth summer job programs, school funding, and the specialized high school entrance exam. The *New York Times* reported that while Teens Take Charge were "ruthless moderators, holding the candidates to the allotted time to answer questions and even cutting them off when necessary," they also made the primary campaign entertaining, engaging candidates in "the first 'truth, dare or dance' round of the 2021 mayoral election season."[2] When none of the candidates opted to dance, Teens Take Charge moderators forced the issue, closing out the segment with the Macarena.

Eric Adams (who was not present for the Macarena dance-off) won the mayoral race. Adams promptly appointed David Banks as his school chancellor. As we have seen, in a sharp departure from the stances of both Chancellor Fariña and Chancellor Carranza, Chancellor Banks argued that efforts to integrate schools or make them more diverse were "playing around on the margins." Harking back to the Bloomberg era, which had deemed integration policies anachronistic, Chancellor Banks explained that his goal was to make all schools excellent, regardless of who attended them. At the same time, grassroots advocacy for integration notably decreased in the wake of the pandemic. The city had long projected a significant drop in student enrollment due to decreased birth rates, which the pandemic exacerbated; in the first two years of the Adams administration, New York City public school enrollment decreased by over one hundred thousand students. Suddenly, it was much easier for many parents to locate seats outside their locally zoned schools. This reality, together with consistent messaging by the NYCDOE that pandemic recovery was the urgent priority, dampened discussions of diversity and integration. New York City schools were not significantly less segregated, but many New Yorkers appeared to have moved on.

Integration and diversity have a long history of moving in and out of public attention. However, this ebb and flow can be misleading. The impacts of school segregation are threaded throughout many education policy debates that do not directly address integration, including analyses of school funding formulas, closure policies, private school vouchers, and standardized test outcomes.[3] These enduring debates illuminate the complicated relationship between student demographics and educational inequality.

The Diverse Lessons We Learn from Diversity

My conversations with students, families, and educators over the years have repeatedly reminded me that the central question is not who goes to school where but how we can make sure that all kids get what they deserve. The same year that I spent my weekdays at P.S. 411 and M.S. 917, I participated in a weekend panel about school integration in New York City. As I listened to other community advocates, educators, and parents debate the most effective ways to diversify our segregated schools, I considered the relationship between policy strategies and social change goals. I wondered if Marquise had really benefited from Hazel's presence in his classroom. I considered how Michelle did and did not learn to fight racism at M.S. 917. I recalled how District 41 staff struggled to help schools locate the resources they urgently needed. Near the end of the conversation, I said to the room, "While I would love for every school to be more racially diverse, diversity is not the goal. The goal is justice. Integration is just one strategy we can use to reach that goal."

The problems that diversity and integration pose for policy and practice are not unique to education; however, these problems become particularly visible in public schools. Pedro Noguera, a sociologist of education, points out that the internal and external constraints structuring school systems are what Paolo Freire would call "limit situations" that require "creative approaches that make it possible to move beyond the dismal status quo."[4] These limit situations require us to look beyond magical solutions, to ask new questions, and to clearly articulate exactly what it is that we are fighting for. As we work toward that collective articulation, the criteria that Du Bois outlined for a quality education can serve as a useful reference point. Every kid deserves access to teachers who demonstrate thoughtful care for their well-being, curricula that reflect their histories and their communities, supportive relationships with their peers, and school facilities that promote learning. Diversity is not on Du Bois's list. That does not mean that integration is unimportant, irrelevant, or, in Chancellor Banks's words, marginal. It simply means that neither diversity nor integration, in and of themselves, signifies movement toward justice. As Du Bois reminds us, the crucial question is not whether kids can be mixed together but what they learn from that mix.

Acknowledging the limits of these racial projects is not a critique of the educators and advocates who work daily to address inequality in our schools and communities. Rather, it is a recognition that this work is very hard, these problems are deeply entrenched, and these individuals, like all of us, are working within limit situations. This is true even in what many people might assume to be the "best case" scenario of New York City: a progressive city with well-funded schools and community-based advocacy for integration. My data demonstrate that diversity-based approaches have inherent constraints. We must acknowledge those constraints if we wish to push against them.

As Jean Anyon wrote in *Radical Possibilities*, "education is an institution whose basic problems are caused by, and whose basic problems reveal, the other crises in cities."[5] Given this fact, the question becomes what diversity-based approaches make possible—and what they foreclose. In each chapter of this book, we have witnessed how various approaches to diversity and integration may fall short of justice. That does not mean that all diversity-based approaches are the same; inside and outside schools, diversity and integration are invoked differently, with important consequences. What individual children learn from these organizations, as well as the ways in which the organizations contribute to broader inequality, varies widely.

The administrators and policy makers of the New York City Department of Education were not responsible for the persistent poverty, residential segregation, and gentrification that characterized District 41. However, they had to respond to it. School and district leaders managed this problem by marketing the potential diversity that they envisioned in district schools, yet they often found themselves limited by market-based approaches. Paradoxically, district staff gained more resources for schools attended by low-income children of color by centering the priorities of "special people": White newcomers to the neighborhood.

At P.S. 411, the outcomes of this white-centered logic were evident in the school's diverging responses to Hazel and Marquise. Staff worked hard to create a diverse school that treated everyone the same, despite the fact that this goal was neither possible nor desirable. Why would we want teachers to ignore the many things that make our children unique? Why would we want educators to lack what Du Bois calls knowledge "not simply of the individual" but also of their surroundings, backgrounds, and community histories? Perhaps if P.S. 411 had set a goal of educators incorporating such knowledge into their daily work, teachers, administrators, and support staff would have recognized how race and class influenced their interpretations of Hazel's and Marquise's behavior, their communication with families, and their allocation of school resources. Perhaps not. It can be challenging for educators to recognize the many ways that schools center White children and their families, reflecting and reproducing the racial inequality that surrounds them. However, it is certainly not possible to interrupt these patterns if the school's objective is to treat everyone the same.

Educators at M.S. 917 believed that schools must do active, against-the-grain, political work to fight racism. They strove to build a truly integrated school and taught their students to do the same. Unlike in P.S. 411, M.S. 917 staff identified the roots of inequality and demonstrated radical care for their students. However, these personal and political relationships were mediated by the standardized approaches fundamental to the grammar of school, in general, and neoliberal choice and accountability-based policies, in particular. Principal Myers strove to "push the limits of public education," teaching students that it was possible for schools to fight racism. Still, the limits of "real school" continued to injure many children—particularly Black children.

Using school walkouts and public testimony, Teens Take Charge members called attention to the injuries that segregation inflicts on New York City students. They demonstrated how segregation prevents children from accessing, in Du Bois's words, the resources and facilities schools need "to induct the child into life." Internally, they tried to create a diverse learning environment predicated on "perfect social equality." However, members like Maimouna mourned the loss of a space led by and for the students who were most directly impacted by school segregation. Like District 41, P.S. 411, and M.S. 917, Teens Take Charge did not fully achieve its goal. Unlike in other organizations, members wrestled publicly with this fact, acknowledging the many ways that the increase in White membership had complicated the organization's goals, strategies, and internal dynamics. These processes, like those I witnessed within the formal educational system, illustrate the trade-offs involved in diverse learning environments.

Unlike District 41 and P.S. 411, Teens Take Charge and M.S. 917 worked for integration, not diversity. Their dedicated efforts managed to interrupt some—but not all—of the racial hierarchies that structure our schools, our education policy system, and our society. Students learned different lessons from the limits and affordances of each space about what they (and we all) deserve. Marquise and his classmates learned from diversity that some students are worthy of protection and resources, while others are not. Michelle and the members of Teens Take Charge learned that while it was their job to interrupt racism, some inequalities cannot be easily interrupted.

These diverging lessons illustrate one simple fact: integration does not magically counter white supremacy. In fact, all too often, diversity can maintain the racial status quo. Whiteness saturates our educational institutions, both formal and informal, and simply celebrating diversity is not going to get us out of that.

No Struggle, No Progress

The first year I taught history at Berkeley High, I posted quotations from historical figures around my classroom walls. Over and over again, our class returned to the famous words of Frederick Douglass: "If there is no struggle, there is no progress. Those who profess to favor freedom, and yet depreciate agitation, are men who want crops without plowing up the ground. They want rain without thunder and lightning. They want the ocean without the awful roar of its many waters. This struggle may be a moral one; or it may be a physical one; or it may be both moral and physical; but it must be a struggle. Power concedes nothing without a demand. It never did and it never will."[6] When I sent Principal Myers a draft of this book to read, he quoted that same passage to me, unaware that I had long ago posted it in my classroom. He explained that "antiracism is a verb": it is something you do and keep doing, whether or not you reach your ultimate goal. What mattered, the principal argued, was the struggle. I agree. But I also believe (and I know Principal Myers does as well) that *how* we struggle has important consequences. In the decade that I have spent on the research for this book, I have repeatedly asked myself how policy makers, educators, and families might work to make schools antiracist, as well as what scholars might learn from their efforts. What exactly are we fighting for? What does it mean to reach beyond what is "practical" toward what we actually want for our children, our communities, and our schools? How might we imagine new possibilities, together? Like many educators and parents, I see these as the most important—and the most difficult—questions to answer. I have only incomplete ideas to offer.

First, let me pause to state the undeniable: educational policy and practice are not individual problems, nor are their failures the responsibility of individual policy makers, educators, parents, or children. At the same time, labeling these problems institutional is an oversimplification. Educational institutions are constituted of individuals. When a child or a family or an educator is unhappy with a school or a school system, they often can point to specific policies or practices, designed and enacted by individual people who could do otherwise. For this reason, we must understand students, families, and staff as policy actors who shape and reshape what is and is not possible, inside and outside schools.

To address both the effects of segregation and the limits of diversity, local policy makers, including elected officials and district administrators, must be willing to make unpopular decisions. The sociologist Casey Stockstill, who studies segregated preschools, writes that segregation "concentrates the effects of structural racism and punishing poverty," contributing to substantial stress among some teachers and students, while enabling others to consider poverty and racism in the US in only abstract terms.[7] Education policies cannot, in and of themselves, negate the effects of white supremacy. However, policies can provide teachers and students access to resources such as smaller classes, a more stable workforce, and better facilities. These tangible resources make it easier for people working in schools to create other intangible resources: classrooms where teachers know and care deeply for their students and develop curricula that address their interests and needs. Rather than focus on selling diversity, policy makers must emphasize these priorities. And in order to achieve these goals, policy makers must intervene in the marketplace, moving beyond, in Carter and Merry's words, "anemic" forms of integration that fail to offer "real equality of opportunity."[8] In other words, policy makers must make justice, rather than diversity or consumer choice, their goal.

I can imagine some parents, educators, or policy makers saying that this would never work in their own communities. They may be right. Across the nation, we have seen pushback from parents who approach schooling as, in Heather McGhee's words, a zero-sum proposition.[9] They worry that changes to school admissions policy will mean that their own children will lose opportunities. This fear is understandable; many Americans have come to see schooling as both a marketplace and a political battlefield.

In conversations about these concerns, I often share that like many parents, I frequently ask myself what is best for my kids. The answer is rarely simple; I have to consider my children's unique characteristics, our family's responsibilities to each other and our community, and the collective future I want us all to build. My partner and I have made a series of very difficult decisions about our own children's schools, and choice policies played a prominent role in our deliberations. We looked for spaces where they would have access to caring teachers and the basic resources schools need to function. We fumed that a good number of New York City public schools do not meet these basic criteria—not because they have low test scores or serve low-income children of color but because they lack the resources they need to do their work well. I am very grateful that my family had the means to find supportive public schools for our sons, one of whom has suffered deeply in school. At the same time, as I tell anyone who will listen, the ongoing effort this requires is emotionally wrenching, absurdly time-consuming, and shockingly inequitable. Over and over, I remind myself, my friends, and my family that my kids do not need or deserve more than anyone else's kids.

As parents and advocates, we can remind policy makers that there is considerable evidence that when education policies become more equitable, communities may hesitate but will eventually accept them. In the past few years, several New York City community school districts have changed admissions policies to allow underserved families greater access to more schools. While these districts faced initial opposition from families who benefited from market-based approaches, these concerns have not persisted.[10] In fact, many families are content to choose among the options presented to them. I think of a friend who enrolled her child in New York City's Gifted and Talented program, despite her concern that it was inequitable, simply because it was a box she could click off on her kindergarten application. If that box had not been present, my friend would not have felt that her child was denied an advantage. It is up to us to demand that policy makers develop options that lead us toward justice, such as controlled choice school admissions.

District 41 administrators tried and failed to use diversity as a lever for equity. How might things have looked different if the district had instead made justice its goal? For one, this approach would relieve the staff of P.S. 411 of the burden of marketing diversity. Instead, school leaders could focus on their most important work: supporting students and teachers. With sufficient time and resources, leaders can encourage teachers to, in Carla Shalaby's words, "imagine our classrooms as free, beautiful places that don't yet exist in the outside world."[11]

Leaders like Principal Blake and Principal Myers could also work with teachers to closely examine what kids learn from school organizational routines, support structures, and labeling and sorting processes. This work is, as Shalaby acknowledges, "unfamiliar and uncomfortable," but it is also necessary.[12] School staff might look long and hard at how resources and recognition are distributed within their schools, considering not just aggregate data but also the meanings that kids like Hazel and Michelle make of diversity. School leaders can create space for teachers to closely examine kids' experience inside their diverse schools, rather than labeling or sorting students.[13] Educators might look systematically at how students interact with each other, classroom curricula, and their teachers; they might, like the staff at M.S. 917, look beyond the walls of their schools to understand their students' communities and histories; they might also listen to Teens Take Charge members describe how and why their most valuable learning often happens outside the classroom. Teachers can then build these new understandings into their curriculum and instruction, recognizing that kids' questions, relationships, and experiences are always central to their learning.[14] Using this approach, integrated classrooms might offer both adults and kids new ways to unlearn racial hierarchies, rather than reinscribe them.

I continue to wonder what it means to participate in the systems we currently have, while reaching for better ones. I witness the impact of our individual and collective choices every day I spend in the field, learning from the students and educators who negotiate, translate, and resist policies they know to be unjust. Diversity poses dilemmas that require us to imagine new possibilities. As one Teens Take Charge member reminded the New York City Council, "Student voice is great, but you know what I prefer? Adult action." Young people like Hazel, Marquise, Michelle, and Maimouna often express their dissatisfaction with the ways we do school, believing that we can and must do better. Adults can do the same.

ACKNOWLEDGMENTS

This book has been a very long time in the making. I am deeply grateful to the varied professional and personal communities that have made completing it possible. While I cannot possibly thank every person who has shared their questions, insights, and knowledge with me here, I am going to do my very best.

First and foremost, I am deeply grateful to the New York City kids, educators, community members, and district staff who graciously shared their experiences with me and welcomed me into their space. I wish I could publicly thank each and every one of you, but as I kept telling you, "confidentiality." You have generously opened up your worlds to me and, in the process, pushed me to fundamentally rethink my assumptions about what diversity can and should mean. Also, you made the process joyful by sharing snacks and silly stories. I particularly want to thank Principal Myers, who offered invaluable detailed comments on a previous draft of this manuscript, and the members of Teens Take Charge, who spent years patiently teaching me about their work.

I have been extremely lucky to learn from many gifted teachers throughout my life who have helped me understand how and why schools work the way they do. Thank you to Pedro Noguera, Lisa Stulberg, and Jim Fraser for your challenging questions and your consistent belief that I could and would find answers through my doctoral studies. Thank you to Dave Donahue, Tomás Galguera, and Anna Richert for anchoring my journey as a teacher and helping me understand my own classroom in particular, as well as public education writ large, as a work in progress. Thank you to my mother for encouraging me to attend to the complicated craft of teaching and for always, always urging me to critically reread my first drafts.

Many people have offered feedback on this book at various points along the way, and I am deeply grateful to each of them. During a manuscript workshop, Thea Abu El-Haj, Maia Cucchiara, John Diamond, and Erica Turner shared encouraging and exacting comments that pushed me to refine my argument. I am particularly grateful to Thea for (as always) urging me to nuance my analysis of the distinct forms that diversity takes, to Erica for encouraging me to name the mess and map out the affordances and limitations of various approaches, to Maia for demanding more ethnographic description, and to John for pointing out that diversity might be neither good nor bad but simply empty. Rachel Fish, who assisted with that workshop, also tirelessly engaged in literal years of close reading and extended text exchanges about each chapter of this book. Elise Castillo, Eve Ewing, Kate Phillippo, Jill Pierce, Sarah Sharp, and Casey Stockstill offered extremely valuable feedback on early chapters when I most needed help. Thanks to each of you, as well as to the students in my Race, Space, and City Schools course at Barnard College—our conversations helped me understand whiteness as an intangible resource in new ways—and to the students in my qualitative research methods courses at UConn: your questions about my methodological choices have revealed a great deal to me as well as (hopefully) you.

My colleagues at the University of Connecticut have consistently advocated for my research. I am particularly thankful for the enthusiastic support of Jennie Weiner and Laura Burton. I am also grateful to the UConn doctoral student Hannah Cooke, who assisted me with cleaning Teens Take Charge data and read some very early writing, and to Alyssa Dillon, Dan Stolzenberg, and Leah Ward, who masterfully administrated logistical support for my research.

Thank you to Jennifer Hammer for making a home for this book at NYU Press and for your unfailing patience with my many questions along the way. Without your careful eye, this book would lack crucial details and include far too many ellipses. Thank you as well to Brianna Jean, Veronica Knutson, and Alexia Traganas of NYU Press for quickly responding to each of my many emails. I am very grateful to two anonymous reviewers offered insightful feedback at several stages of the project, which have very much improved the book. Thank you to Laura Portwood-Stacer for your sharp feedback on my book proposal and your on-point responses to my questions about the publication process. And thank you to Dulce M. Marquez for your amazing photographs of Teens Take Charge, which I have known I wanted to include in my book since the first time I saw them. I am also grateful to the *Harvard Education Review* for generously granting permission to incorporate material from an article I had previously published in that journal into chapter 2.

This work would not have been possible without generous support from several foundations and institutions. The Spencer Foundation offered crucial funding at several points for the research reported in this book, including a research grant (#202300176), a National Academy of Education/Spencer Foundation Dissertation Fellowship, and a National Academy of Education/Spencer Foundation Research Development Award. The views expressed are my own and do not necessarily reflect the views of the Spencer Foundation. I also received support from the Fahs-Beck Fund for Social Research and the NYU Steinhardt Mitchell Leaska Dissertation Award during the initial phases of this project. Funding from Seton Hall University supported my work with Teens Take Charge and the UConn Scholarship Facilitation Fund supported costs associated with publishing this book. I am very grateful to each of these funders for their support.

There is no way I could have written this book without child care. During a global pandemic, Janitza Ramirez played innumerable games of Uno with my children, patiently helped them log on to Zoom school, and, when all else failed, took them to the playground to find popsicles. The work of teachers is infinitely more than babysitting, but I was so grateful when they returned to school. I am particularly thankful to John Allgood, Kristina Davis, Rachel Hutchison, Nancy Larsen, Hannah Stark, and Alex Stimmel for teaching my kids to care for their neighbors, to ask challenging questions, and to find answers in their communities, within and beyond their classrooms.

Thank you to the many wise, caring, and committed colleagues and friends who have offered thoughtful feedback on my rawest ideas, asked and answered late-night questions, and given me chocolate along the way. Ricky Blissett, Sarah Diem, Rachel Fish, Laura Mauldin, Jill Pierce, Rachel Silver, Erica Turner, and Adriana Villavicencio, you model engaged scholarship and inspire me to rethink what my work can look like. I am very grateful. Sarah Boyce, Hallie Chertok, Jenn Cole, Celia Garner, Heather McKay, and Sarah Sharp, you have celebrated my successes, helped me recover from my failures, and fed my family over the decade that this project took shape. I cannot wait to cook you all a meal.

I spent too much time thinking about whether to place my family first or last in these acknowledgments. They are the beginning and the ending, and I am deeply grateful for each of them. My parents, Helen and Stephen Freidus, taught me to always ask why and how the world is the way it is, while expressing deep care for the people in it. Your confidence in my capacity to take on challenging, worthwhile tasks and your love for the written word made this book possible. Although my father died as I was drafting this book, his pride in my work continues to sustain me. My sister, Tasha, has spent her life demonstrating that caring for others and striving for change can be joyful work. Thank you for your hugs and jokes, even the bad puns. I could not ask for better in-laws than Gloria and Gerry Scorse; thank you for the amazing rapidity with which you offer a helping hand and your consistent encouragement of our entire family. Dan, I cannot begin to list the many ways you have loved, celebrated, and supported me and my work; please know that I am thinking of them all when I thank you. Ari and Lew, thank you for the righteous indignation you express at injustice, your impatience for the world to be otherwise, and your expectation that we can change it. We will build that new world together.

APPENDIX

Methodological Reflections

I came to this project with questions that had been nagging at me for over a decade, since I worked in first highly segregated and then highly diverse California public schools. My questions became more intense when I moved to New York City. I wanted to know why it was so hard to find racially and socioeconomically diverse schools in New York, compared to the San Francisco Bay Area (which is not to say that there is no segregation in the Bay Area—simply that it is less extreme). I frequently combed through publicly available demographic data in search of diverse schools. At times, I was not sure if I was looking for potential research sites or future schools for my own child; I found few that fell into either category.

During my first two years of doctoral studies, I tried out different ways of understanding school policy and practice in our segregated city. As I pored over court documents detailing the contentious history of New York City school desegregation orders, I began to understand the relationship between the Bloomberg administration's market-based reforms and its indifference about school segregation.[1] Digging deep in the archives of parent listservs, I connected how people talked about public schools to their perceptions of local neighborhoods.[2] Relatively quickly, I realized that if I wanted to study school diversity in New York City, I would have to also study gentrification, because the handful of racially and socioeconomically diverse schools were almost always located in gentrifying areas of the city. Over the course of two semesters under the guidance of Lisa Stulberg and Caitlin Zaloom, I conducted fieldwork in several schools. These class projects hooked me on ethnography.

They also helped me articulate new questions about how race, class, and power intersect in diversifying schools and the implications of changing school demographics for classroom teaching and learning.

HOPES AND FEARS: HOW COMMUNITIES TALK ABOUT DIVERSIFYING SCHOOLS

I spent 2015–18 working on a multisited ethnography of gentrifying schools and communities. Because I wanted to understand how the ways people talked about school diversity were and were not related to what actually happens in diverse schools, I spent my first year of data collection observing meetings and other public discourse in District 41. I chose District 41 for several important reasons: it was rapidly gentrifying; it had been the site of public conversation about school demographics for several years; and the superintendent welcomed me there, encouraging staff to talk with me and introducing me to the principals of several schools. Although District 41 was, of course, unique, it was not an outlier. The dilemmas, deliberations, and initiatives the district engaged in closely resembled five other gentrifying community school districts within the NYCDOE.

During my first year of fieldwork, I focused primarily on the hopes and fears that District 41 community members expressed about diversifying schools. I spent that year gathering as many types of data as possible. I attended thirty-four meetings that addressed diversity in the district that year. Many of these meetings were public, including town halls about the rezoning of P.S. 411, district diversity workshops, and Community Education Council (CEC) meetings, where elected parent members discussed local schools and what the district could do to support them. I also occasionally observed public meetings in similar community school districts, in order to see how their conversations were similar to and different from those of District 41. Superintendent Arnett invited me to join district leadership team and diversity committee meetings, as well as additional staff meetings on related topics. During each observation, I jotted notes recording phrases, interactions, and observations; I wrote up detailed field notes as quickly as possible when the meeting ended, but always within twenty-four hours. I recorded and paid for transcription of some public meetings, when so much was being said that I wanted to capture every single word. I also closely tracked discussions of District 41 in local news and social media, paying careful attention to how people talked about school and district policy in interviews and the voluminous comments responding to each post or article. I owe a particular debt to local coverage of school integration advocacy in *Chalkbeat* and the *School Colors* podcast, supplemented by more mainstream publications such as the *New York Times*, the *Daily News*, and the *New York Post*. When I quote a person directly in this book, it comes from an interview I conducted, a field note I took verbatim during an observation, an audio transcript of a public meeting, or one of these media sources. I identify the context for each quotation in the narrative.

After I had spent about six months gathering these data, I interviewed eight district staff, CEC members, and community volunteers about their views of what was happening in the district. By the time I began these interviews, none of these people were strangers. After months of sitting together in meeting rooms, we met at coffee shops and front stoops, talking about diversity and segregation in District 41. Our conversations sounded much more like discussions between friends or associates, rather than formal interviews. Initially, this dismayed me as I played back the audio recordings; I worried that I had talked too much or that the interviews did not sound serious enough. Later, I came to see these interactions as a sign of the reciprocal relationships we had developed over time.

Over the course of my fieldwork, many aspects of my own social location changed. I went from having one child to having two; I conducted a significant portion of district fieldwork while first visibly pregnant and then bringing an infant with me to committee meetings. (My decision to spend a year focused on district context was also related to the timing of my pregnancy.) In the spring of 2015, as I sat through district meetings about families' school preferences, it was time for my own family to enter the elementary school lottery. The following fall, my older son entered kindergarten. I spent much of my time that year in a kindergarten classroom at P.S. 411, thinking of my kid as I watched Hazel and Marquise struggle with school.

How I perceived others and how I was perceived shifted considerably during this period, especially given that I was more or less visibly a mother at various points in time. But some things stayed the same. I was consistently recognized as a White woman and a relative newcomer to New York City, studying diversity in gentrifying schools. While my graduate student status made me appear less powerful to some people, I was also a former educator and future professor. These overlapping personal and professional identities mattered in different ways to different people. I paid careful attention to moments when people in the field explicitly commented on my professional roles or social locations, and I also looked for more implicit moments in which they positioned me or I positioned myself relative to the school community. I came to think about myself as neither an insider nor an outsider but as shifting inside and outside of specific social settings. I also came to see my various social locations—and the power or lack thereof that resulted from them—as relative and variable, depending on the scene, the people, and the interaction. This was a useful approach to keep in mind once I began fieldwork in schools.

INSIDE THE BLACK BOX: TEACHING AND LEARNING IN DIVERSIFYING SCHOOLS

In addition to understanding how community members think about diversifying schools, I wanted to know what happened inside them. How did the school staff perceive neighborhood newcomers? How did teachers and school leaders respond to their changing student body? How did students perceive each other? What did a racially and socioeconomically diverse group of students learn from their school and from their classmates?

I spent the 2016–17 school year investigating these questions in two schools: P.S. 411 and M.S. 917. As with most school ethnographies, the challenge of access played a large role in my site selection. Superintendent Arnett introduced me via email to principals at several schools in District 41; while he did not put any pressure on them to allow me to conduct research, he did endorse my project. When I followed up with Principal Blake, she decided it would be interesting to have me at P.S. 411—as long as a teacher offered to host me in their class. Because the younger grades at P.S. 411 were the most diverse, I reached out to all the kindergarten and first-grade teachers to see if they were willing for me to observe, explaining that I would be happy to help out in return by preparing classroom materials or performing administrative tasks. One teacher in each grade level expressed interest. I decided that Ms. O'Shea's kindergarten classroom was the best fit because she was highly regarded at the school and it offered me the opportunity to watch students transition into P.S. 411.

My entry to M.S. 917 was somewhat different. Because sixth-grade students moved as cohorts from classroom to classroom, I needed to observe multiple teachers each day. Principal Myers informed all the sixth-grade teachers that I would be observing one cohort of kids that year. Some staff appeared eager to have me there; some appeared indifferent; nobody acted hostile or gave me reason to believe they were uncomfortable with my presence. A few teachers remembered me from when I had conducted pilot observations during the first year that a group of White sixth graders had enrolled at the school.

I typically spent two or three days a week at each school that year, for a total of sixty-five observation days at M.S. 917 and fifty-one days at P.S. 411. Sometimes I was there for the entire school day and wrote up my field notes later that evening; on other days, I spent only the morning at school and left around lunchtime to record my notes. I sometimes found it tempting to focus my attention on teachers during class observations. However, I reminded myself to focus on students whenever possible. My professional experience had taught me that kids, like adults, play important roles in constructing and reconstructing racial projects. As a teacher, as a professional development facilitator, and during my pilot fieldwork, I had observed the truth of Hugh Mehan's words: "Students, like teachers, have objectives that they would like to meet during the course of a given classroom event, a school day, a school year. And, like teachers, students employ others and their surroundings as contexts for achieving these objectives."[3] I developed a lot of respect for students and their strategies. That respect is one reason why I generally call them "kids," rather than "children," since that is the language students themselves used.

While I was not perceived as a teacher at either school—at P.S. 411, kids called me "Ms. Alex," a naming convention they reserved for assistants and volunteers, while M.S. 917 kids just called me "Alex"—I still retained adult authority. Kindergarteners were quick to ask me for help tying their shoes, and sixth graders often turned to me when they did not understand an assignment, despite my attempts to encourage kids to work through challenges on their own (a very adult strategy, to be honest). Their refusal to separate me from my grown-up status was entirely justified. I was free to move across the room if I wanted to see something or linger in the hallways after class began, chatting with staff. In fact, P.S. 411 teachers frequently welcomed me in their classrooms precisely *because* they wanted the presence of another adult. These teachers looked at me with evident disapproval if I did not discipline children who broke rules in my presence. After a few weeks, it became obvious that my attempt to evade authority was straining my relationships with school staff. On my commute home from P.S. 411 one day, I remembered reading about this tension in Amanda Lewis's *Race in the Schoolyard*. I looked it up and decided that, like Lewis, I would try to align myself with kids while occasionally reminding them of classroom norms by making comments like, "We are all going to get in trouble."[4] I also sought out opportunities to sit with students in small groups or one on one, which allowed me to observe students up close while easing teachers' workloads.

In November, I completed initial interviews with teachers at both schools. That winter, I interviewed students (six of eighteen students in the focal classroom at P.S. 411 and fourteen of twenty-five students in the focal cohort at M.S. 917). The following spring, I interviewed a cross-section of staff members at each site (ten teachers, administrators, and counselors at P.S. 411 and eleven teachers, administrators, and paraprofessionals at M.S. 917), as well as Hazel and Marquise's mothers at P.S. 411. I also conducted a student focus group at M.S. 917 that spring.

While researchers sometimes talk about "gaining access" as a one-time event, I experienced it as an extended process. Every time I paused for a quick conversation with a kid in the hallway or invited someone to an interview was a moment in which I was asking for access. It took a long time for some people, especially some M.S. 917 students, to become accustomed to my presence. At the beginning of the school year, I introduced myself to the sixth graders several times, and I answered questions as they came up that fall. Still, one day in late November, a student asked what I did all day at school. Jayden, who was listening to our conversation, piped up: "She takes notes." When I smiled and confirmed that it was true, I mostly took notes, the student asked me why. Before I could answer, Jayden again answered for me: "for the government." My jaw dropped, and I rushed to correct him. Jayden and the other kids appeared to believe my explanation, but I was reminded once again that relationships can take a long time to develop.

Like other school ethnographers, I sometimes found myself drawing on my adult identities as a former teacher and a mother as I interacted with students.[5] As a White mother who lived in a recently gentrified neighborhood, I was highly attuned to racialized interactions among kids and adults. As a former high school teacher, I was fully aware of the challenges of working in public schools. Inspired by the approach of the sociologist Sarah Lawrence-Lightfoot, I tried to be both "generous and tough, skeptical and receptive," as I observed classrooms.[6] Ultimately, like Lawrence-Lightfoot, I decided to develop portraits of several students and their schools.[7]

Staff at both P.S. 411 and M.S. 917 seemed to alternately see me as an observer, as a colleague, and as a parent. Over the course of the school year, I became friendly with many teachers as we ate lunch together in empty classrooms; sometimes we talked about how class was going, but at other times, we chatted about our families or city politics. I also developed close relationships with a few sixth graders who asked for advice on personal questions. I was aware that power differences between myself and the people I studied probably influenced our interactions. As my fieldwork progressed, I looked for raced and gendered patterns in these relationships, wondering whether it was easier for me to develop informal relationships with students and teachers who were more like myself. That did not generally appear to be the case, although I did note that several Black and Latine boys at M.S. 917 took longer to seem comfortable with my presence in the classroom. (For example, Jayden, who had been so sure I worked for the government, was a Black kid.)

As I observed and interviewed participants, I wrote regular reflective memos about the significance of events, initial interpretations of emerging patterns, and particular moments that I wanted to explore in more depth. Teachers and students were curious about my responses to classroom events and occasionally asked what I noticed. When I was comfortable doing so, I shared my impressions, and we unpacked them together, noting the ways my perspectives overlapped with or diverged from their own. These conversations offered space for kids and adults to challenge my analyses and share their own interpretations of events.

STUDENT ACTIVISTS: LEARNING AND ORGANIZING IN TEENS TAKE CHARGE

The year I spent at P.S. 411 and M.S. 917 left me simultaneously grateful for educators' hard work and saddened by the structural inequality that saturates our classrooms. When the project wrapped up, I decided to take a break from what happens inside schools. I looked instead to how advocates—especially teen activists—were influencing New York City educational policy. I wondered how these young people made sense of their experiences in the city's segregated schools. I also wanted to know what they learned from their advocacy and whether working outside of classrooms made new kinds of learning possible.

I had followed Teens Take Charge in local media for several years. In July 2019, I got in touch with Taylor, the sole adult Teens Take Charge staff member, who then asked a youth leader to talk with me and decide whether or not to allow me to observe. I was impressed that a youth leader was given this authority, but Teens Take Charge seemed to regard it as a relatively low-stakes decision. Because members were so accustomed to reporters and potential funders observing their work, the organization was not particularly worried about an additional person in the room or keeping the group's identity anonymous. In fact, many of their meetings and protests that fall were recorded for a documentary film. This is why they are the only organization in this book that I refer to by name; after prolonged reflection, I decided that it was simply not possible to deidentify Teens Take Charge, given the highly public nature of their work. It seemed intellectually dishonest to attempt (and probably fail) to mask the group's identity.[8] I made this decision in consultation with both my university Institutional Review Board and the Teens Take Charge leadership team. I took a very different approach in schools. I did my best to keep the identities of District 41, P.S. 411, and M.S. 917 confidential; I used pseudonyms and altered a few potentially identifying details for each organization. I also changed names and identifying details for individuals, such as school and district staff, parents, and students (including Teens Take Charge members). The only individuals whom I name are public figures such as Mayor de Blasio and Chancellor Fariña.

I spent September 2019 through July 2020 following Teens Take Charge members from strategy sessions to rallies to meetings with the NYCDOE, first in person and then, after the city locked down due to the coronavirus outbreak in March 2020, on Zoom. I observed them once or twice each week, in small and large groups, for a total of fifty-six field observations. As always, I jotted notes as I observed and expanded those jottings into full field notes within twenty-four hours of each observation. Because many events were reported in local media, I also referred to news clips and articles to supplement my data. Teens Take Charge also granted me access to many of its internal documents and WhatsApp groups, which were an invaluable resource for understanding how the group worked. I did occasionally have to remind members that I had access to the group chat, so they should be careful not to share anything there that they did not want me to read.

After months of informal conversations in the field, I interviewed thirty-five Teens Take Charge members between December 2019 and July 2020, some in person and some on Zoom. I talked with a wide range of people; eighteen interviewees had been youth leaders at some point, while the remaining half were members who participated less consistently. Ten of the people I interviewed identified as Black or African American, ten as Latine or Hispanic, nine as White, five as Asian American, and one as Middle Eastern; this roughly reflected the group's demographics during the year that I observed. The majority of the people I interviewed, like the majority of Teens Take Charge members, were young women.

I appreciated members' sharp political analyses and warm community, even as I noted tensions within the group. The field notes and memos I wrote after each interview reflected how much I enjoyed spending time with them. Over the course of the year, I became particularly friendly with a few youth leaders. Before meetings, we ate pizza and chatted about music, high school homework, and college applications; after meetings, we rode the subway together and reflected on the evening's events. Several members told me that they felt validated by how seriously I took their work.

I never felt like an insider at Teens Take Charge. Although members knew that I, too, had advocated for changes to New York City enrollment policies, they also knew that my experience was quite different from theirs in many ways. They were very clear on the ways that my adult status, as well as my repeated signals that I would not take a stance on internal organizational debates, separated me from the group. In some moments, this seemed to increase distance between us; in others, it seemed to allow people to see me as a trusted confidante. I noticed that most White members appeared relatively comfortable with me from the outset, and a few (but not most) members of color did not. I spent a lot of time in informal conversations with these members, explaining my research goals and sharing resources, which seemed to help considerably.

I periodically asked myself and Teens Take Charge members how my experiences as a White woman, a mother, and a former teacher may have shaped my perceptions and interpretations of interactions and comments. They were happy to help me think these questions through. I rechecked quotations and conclusions with members a year after I completed my fieldwork, as I started writing about the group. In 2023, I also conducted a round of follow-up interviews with twenty-five of the thirty-five people I originally interviewed, as well as two focus groups in which they reflected together on their shared experiences. In some of these follow-up conversations, members had shifted their interpretations of events or relationships; I accounted for those evolving perspectives in the analyses I share in chapter 4. These ongoing conversations with TTC members made me much more confident in my findings.

PUTTING THE PUZZLE PIECES TOGETHER

In some ways, spending time in four different places limited what I could learn from each setting. I probably would have gathered more data at each site if I had not moved among them. However, the extended and multisited nature of this project also allowed me to develop analyses I might otherwise have missed.

While a great deal of my analysis took place during and immediately following each wave of data collection, some of my most important insights happened as I looked from site to site. There was no way for me to assess the validity of local hopes and fears about school diversity without gathering data from schools. If I had not been going back and forth each week between M.S. 917 and P.S. 411, I might not have paid as careful attention to differences between the two principals' leadership styles and staff approaches to their work. Examining how sixth graders entered M.S. 917 also helped me notice children's transition to kindergarten at P.S. 411 in a different light. And watching the lessons Michelle learned at M.S. 917 helped me articulate new questions about how learning might and might not be different outside of school, which led me to Teens Take Charge. Looking across these sites offered opportunities to identify patterns that I would not have identified on my own.

This study began with a specific puzzle: extreme school segregation in one of the nation's most racially and economically diverse cities. A multisited study offered the opportunity to examine the puzzle from multiple angles, noticing overlaps and disjunctures in what I observed, what happened in different spaces, and what prior research has found. Context always matters in educational policy and practice; these particular spaces in this particular city are, of course, unique. However, the underlying tensions that inform the racial projects of diversity and integration are not limited to these sites. Rather than taking a purely inductive or deductive approach, I focused on how theoretical work helped me understand these cases and on how these cases could help us nuance and extend existing theory. My hope is that by better understanding how these tensions affect kids, schools, and communities, we can reimagine new paths toward justice.

NOTES

INTRODUCTION

1. Freidus and Noguera, "From 'Good Will' to 'Anachronism.'"
2. Veiga, "Chancellor Richard Carranza Stands by His Tweet."
3. Meckler, "NYC's Black Schools Chief."
4. Du Bois, "Does the Negro Need Separate Schools?," 328.
5. Diamond, "Defending the Color Line"; Ladson-Billings, "Landing on the Wrong Note."
6. Brown v. Board of Education, 347 U.S. 483, 494 (1954).
7. Diamond, "Defending the Color Line."
8. Johnson, *Children of the Dream*.
9. Lewis and Diamond, *Despite the Best Intentions*; Noguera and Wing, *Unfinished Business*.
10. Horsford, *Learning in a Burning House*; Dumas, "Against the Dark"; Posey-Maddox et al., "Black Parents' Educational Decision-Making."
11. Carter, *Stubborn Roots*. See also Wells et al., *Both Sides Now*; Schneider et al., "Student Experience Outcomes."
12. Oakes, *Keeping Track*; Tyson, *Integration Interrupted*; Gregory, Skiba, and Noguera, "Achievement Gap and the Discipline Gap."
13. Hagerman, *White Kids*; Lewis, *Race in the Schoolyard*; Abu El-Haj, *Elusive Justice*; Ochoa, *Academic Profiling*.
14. Omi and Winant, *Racial Formation in the United States*, 56.
15. Omi and Winant, 55.
16. Kahlenberg, *All Together Now*; Wells, Fox, and Cordova-Coba, *How Racially Diverse Schools*; Frankenberg and Orfield, *Lessons in Integration*.
17. Dumas, "Against the Dark"; ross, *On the Road to Brown and Beyond*. Scholars disagree on whether and when to capitalize terms used to describe race. In this book, I have chosen to capitalize "White" and "Black" when describing individuals or groups of people. I leave the terms uncapitalized when they refer to abstract ideas or systems, such as "white supremacy" and "antiblackness."
18. Jackson, *Life in Classrooms*; Anyon, "Social Class"; Shalaby, *Troublemakers*.
19. Du Bois, "Does the Negro Need Separate Schools?," 330.
20. D. Cohen, *NYC School Segregation Report Card*; Kucsera and Orfield, *New York State's Extreme School Segregation*.
21. Bonastia, *Battle Nearer to Home*.

22 Theoharris, *More Beautiful and Terrible History*; Delmont, *Why Busing Failed*.
23 D. Cohen, *NYC School Segregation Report Card*; Kucsera and Orfield, *New York State's Extreme School Segregation*.
24 Hemphill and Mader, *Segregated Schools in Integrated Neighborhoods*; Cordova-Cobo and Ellen, *State of New York City's Housing and Neighborhoods*; Mordechay and Ayscue, *School Integration in Gentrifying Neighborhoods*.
25 Solórzano and Yosso, "Critical Race Methodology," 26; Ewing, *Ghosts in the Schoolyard*.
26 Lipman, *New Political Economy of Urban Education*.
27 Weis and Fine, "Critical Bifocality and Circuits of Privilege," 196.
28 Ball et al., "Policy Subjects and Policy Actors in Schools."
29 Phillippo, *Contest without Winners*.
30 McDermott, "Acquisition of a Child"; Shalaby, *Troublemakers*; Mehan, "Competent Student"; Lareau, *Unequal Childhoods*; Pattillo, *Black on the Block*.
31 Mehan, "Understanding Inequality in Schools," 3.
32 Ewing, *Ghosts in the Schoolyard*, 13.
33 Pawlewicz, "Teacher Blame."
34 Starck et al., "Teachers Are People Too."
35 Kendi, *How to Be an Antiracist*, 10.
36 Diamond, "Defending the Color Line."
37 powell, "New Theory of Integrated Education," 298.

1. "WE WEREN'T SPECIAL TO HIM"

1 I have used pseudonyms throughout this book to protect the privacy of the people involved. I have also slightly altered some specifics (such as a child's precise age or details about a neighborhood) and public data that might identify individuals.
2 Cucchiara, *Marketing Schools, Marketing Cities*.
3 Noguera and Syeed, *City Schools and the American Dream* 2.
4 C. Cohen, *Democracy Remixed*, 11.
5 Lipman, *New Political Economy of Urban Education*, 10–11.
6 Orfield, foreword to *New York State's Extreme School Segregation*, iii.
7 Hemphill and Mader, *Segregated Schools in Integrated Neighborhoods*; Cordova-Cobo and Ellen, *State of New York City's Housing and Neighborhoods*.
8 Mader, Hemphill, and Abbas, *Paradox of Choice*.
9 Mordechay and Ayscue, *White Growth, Persistent Segregation*.
10 Orfield, foreword to *New York State's Extreme School Segregation*, v.
11 Cucchiara, *Marketing Schools, Marketing Cities*; Posey-Maddox, *When Middle-Class Parents Choose Urban Schools*; Syeed, "There Goes the PTA."
12 Bischoff and Tach, "School Choice, Neighborhood Change"; Orfield and Frankenberg and Associates, *Educational Delusions?*; Gordon, *This Is Our School!*
13 Charter school enrollment lotteries are a parallel, concurrent, yet separate process that is not administered by NYCDOE.

14 Roda and Wells, "School Choice Policies and Racial Segregation"; Sattin-Bajaj and Roda, "Opportunity Hoarding."
15 Lipman, *New Political Economy of Urban Education*; Gordon, *This Is Our School!*; Brown-Saracino, *Neighborhood That Never Changes*.
16 Cucchiara, *Marketing Schools, Marketing Cities*.
17 Russo, "Upper West Side School Rezoning Proposal."
18 Wall, "De Blasio."
19 One way to understand the role of real estate and parents' feelings of entitlement to specific schools is through Cheryl Harris's foundational argument that whiteness functions as a form of property in US society and the legal system ("Whiteness as Property"). For further discussion of this argument in relation to the events in District 41, please see my article "Modes of Belonging."
20 Gill, "Farina."
21 Pierce, "Official Approaches to Equity and Democracy."
22 Cucchiara, *Marketing Schools, Marketing Cities*; Gordon, *This Is Our School!*; Quarles and Butler, "Toward a Multivocal Research Agenda"; Posey-Maddox, *When Middle-Class Parents Choose Urban Schools*.
23 Bell and Hartmann, "Diversity in Everyday Discourse."
24 Turner, "Marketing Diversity."
25 Berrey, *Enigma of Diversity*, 174.
26 Delmont, *Why Busing Failed*.
27 Zimmer and Hurowitz, "Schools Boss Touts Pen Pal System"; Bonastia, *Battle Nearer to Home*, 26.
28 Zimmerman, "Fariña to Parents."
29 School Diversity Advisory Group, *Making the Grade*, 24.
30 New York City Department of Education, "Diversity in Our Schools."
31 Melamed, "Spirit of Neoliberalism."
32 Parents Involved in Community Schools v. Seattle School District No. 1, 551 U.S. 701, 748 (2007).
33 New York State Education Department, "2015–18 Title I School Improvement Section 1003(a) Socioeconomic Integration Pilot Program," 1.
34 Orfield, foreword to *NYC School Segregation Report Card*.
35 Gordon, *This Is Our School!*; Lipman, "Cultural Politics."
36 Ewing, *Ghosts in the Schoolyard*, 10.
37 Carter and Welner, *Closing the Opportunity Gap*; Ladson-Billings, "From the Achievement Gap to the Education Debt."
38 Wells, "Process of Racial Resegregation," 4.
39 Posey-Maddox, *When Middle-Class Parents Choose Urban Schools*, 37.
40 Freidus, "Great School Benefits Us All"; Cucchiara, *Marketing Schools, Marketing Cities*; Turner, *Suddenly Diverse*.
41 Evans, "I Wanted Diversity, but Not So Much."

42 Menken, Espinet, and Avni, "There Was Nothing Here," 449.
43 Berrey, *Enigma of Diversity*, 178.
44 Turner, "Marketing Diversity," 812.
45 Turner, *Suddenly Diverse*.
46 Lewis and Diamond, *Despite the Best Intentions*.
47 Cucchiara, *Marketing Schools, Marketing Cities*; Posey-Maddox, *When Middle-Class Parents Choose Urban Schools*.
48 Berrey, *Enigma of Diversity*, 7.
49 Turner, "Marketing Diversity," 812.
50 Du Bois, "Does the Negro Need Separate Schools?"
51 Anyon, *Ghetto Schooling*, 168.
52 Nygreen, *These Kids*, 50.

2. PROBLEM CHILDREN AND CHILDREN WITH PROBLEMS

This chapter incorporates data and analyses that first appeared in my article "'Problem Children' and 'Children with Problems,'" originally published in *Harvard Educational Review* 90, no. 4 (2020).

1 Cucchiara, *Marketing Schools, Marketing Cities*.
2 Carter, *Stubborn Roots*; Fish, "Racialized Construction of Exceptionality"; Owens, "Double Jeopardy."
3 Ramey, "Social Structure."
4 Hatt, "Smartness as a Cultural Practice in Schools"; Mehan, "Competent Student"; Shalaby, *Troublemakers*.
5 MacLure et al., "Becoming a Problem," 448.
6 Musto, "Brilliant or Bad"; Shalaby, *Troublemakers*; Thorne, *Gender Play*.
7 Wortham, *Learning Identity*.
8 Freidus, "'Problem Children' and 'Children with Problems.'"
9 Ridgeway, "Framed before We Know It."
10 Carter Andrews et al., "Impossibility of Being 'Perfect and White'"; Crenshaw, "Mapping the Margins"; Deliovsky, "Normative White Femininity."
11 Zimmermann, "Penalty of Being a Young Black Girl"; Epstein, Blake, and González, *Girlhood Interrupted*, 20.
12 Nelson, "Relationships of (Re)Imagining," 125.
13 Goff et al., "Essence of Innocence"; Ferguson, *Bad Boys*.
14 Stockstill, *False Starts*.
15 Ferguson, *Bad Boys*; Gilliam et al., "Early Educators' Implicit Biases."
16 Dobbs, Arnold, and Doctoroff, "Attention in the Preschool Classroom"; Erden and Wolfgang, "Exploration of the Differences in Prekindergarten."
17 Annamma, "Whiteness as Property."
18 Diamond and Gomez, "Disrupting White Supremacy," 4.
19 Diamond and Lewis, "Race and Discipline."
20 Ferguson, *Bad Boys*; Noguera, *Trouble with Black Boys*.

21 Carter Andrews et al., "Impossibility of Being 'Perfect and White.'"
22 Berrey, *Enigma of Diversity*, 41.
23 Elliott and Bowen, "Defending Motherhood."
24 Nelson, "Relationships of (Re)Imagining"; Valenzuela, *Subtractive Schooling*.
25 Shalaby, *Troublemakers*, 153.
26 Caraballo, "Being 'Loud'"; Musto, "Brilliant or Bad"; Nygreen, *These Kids*; Shange, *Progressive Dystopia*.
27 Diamond and Lewis, "Race and Discipline," 18.
28 Allport, *Nature of Prejudice*, 264.
29 Du Bois, "Does the Negro Need Separate Schools?," 328.
30 Elwert, Keller, and Kotsadam, "Rearranging the Desk Chairs"; Fine, Weis, and Powell, "Communities of Difference."
31 Carter and Merry, "Wall to Wall," 19.
32 Abu El-Haj, *Elusive Justice*; Pollock, *Colormute*; Shange, *Progressive Dystopia*.
33 Lewis and Diamond, *Despite the Best Intentions*, 8.

3. WHAT IS TAUGHT AND WHAT IS LEARNED

1 Noguera and Wing, *Unfinished Business*; Meier, Stewart, and England, *Race, Class, and Education*; Lewis and Diamond, *Despite the Best Intentions*.
2 Irby, *Stuck Improving*.
3 Tyack and Cuban, *Tinkering toward Utopia*; Tyack and Tobin, "'Grammar' of Schooling."
4 Tyack and Tobin, "'Grammar' of Schooling," 454.
5 Mehta, "Possible Futures."
6 Labaree, "Dynamic Tension," 30.
7 Mehta, "Possible Futures."
8 Dumas, "Against the Dark"; Diamond and Gomez, "Disrupting White Supremacy"; Shange, *Progressive Dystopia*.
9 Sojoyner, *First Strike*, xi.
10 Gregory, Skiba, and Noguera, "Achievement Gap and the Discipline Gap"; Diamond and Lewis, "Opportunity Hoarding."
11 V. Ray, "Theory of Racialized Organizations."
12 ross, "Black Space in Education," 48–50.
13 Rivera-McCutchen, *Radical Care*.
14 Siddle-Walker, *Their Highest Potential*.
15 Pascoe, *Nice Is Not Enough*.
16 Metz, "Real School."
17 Castillo, "Neoliberal Grammar of Schooling?," 538.
18 Wortham, *Learning Identity*.
19 Kao and Joyner, "Do Race and Ethnicity Matter among Friends?"; Pica-Smith, "Children Speak about Interethnic and Interracial Friendships."
20 Carter, *Stubborn Roots*.

21 Carter, 92; Wells, Fox, and Cordova-Coba, *How Racially Diverse Schools*; Schneider et al., "Student Experience Outcomes."
22 Dumas, "Against the Dark"; Shange, *Progressive Dystopia*.
23 Ladson-Billings, "Toward a Theory of Culturally Relevant Pedagogy."
24 Ladson-Billings, "Culturally Relevant Pedagogy 2.0."
25 Royal and Gibson, "They Schools."
26 Freidus, "I Didn't Have a Lesson."
27 Du Bois, "Does the Negro Need Separate Schools?"
28 Holloway and Brass, "Making Accountable Teachers"; Au, "Teaching under the New Taylorism."
29 Metz, "Real School," 78.
30 Lipman, *High Stakes Education*, 3.
31 Holloway and Brass, "Making Accountable Teachers," 378–80.
32 Royal and Gibson, "They Schools," 14.
33 Ladson-Billings, "Toward a Theory of Culturally Relevant Pedagogy," 478.
34 Noguera and Wing, *Unfinished Business*; Lewis and Diamond, *Despite the Best Intentions*; Irby, *Stuck Improving*.
35 Morris, "'Ladies' or 'Loudies'?"; Carter Andrews et al., "Impossibility of Being 'Perfect and White.'"
36 Shange, *Progressive Dystopia*, 115.
37 Abu El-Haj, *Elusive Justice*, 127.
38 Paris and Alim, "What Are We Seeking to Sustain?," 86.
39 Fish, "Racialized Construction of Exceptionality"; Owens, "Double Jeopardy"; Tenenbaum and Ruck, "Are Teachers' Expectations Different?"
40 Hagerman, "Racial Ideology and White Youth," 329.
41 R. Ray, "School as a Hostile Institution"; Ferguson, *Bad Boys*.
42 Dumas, "Beginning and Ending with Black Suffering," 30.
43 powell, "New Theory of Integrated Education."
44 For more on the importance of principals' beliefs and agency in navigating institutional constraints, see McGhee and Anderson, "Gentrification, Market Regimes, and the New Entrepreneurial Principal."
45 Mehta and Datnow, "Changing the Grammar of Schooling"; Cohen and Mehta, "Why Reform Sometimes Succeeds."
46 De Royston et al., "Rethinking Schools, Rethinking Learning," 5.
47 Nasir et al., "Rethinking Learning," 562.
48 Castagno, *Educated in Whiteness*; R. Ray, "Race-Conscious Racism."
49 Shange, *Progressive Dystopia*, 93.
50 Tyack and Tobin, "'Grammar' of Schooling," 478.

4. "A TRUE HISTORY OF AMERICA"

1 Baldridge, *Reclaiming Community*, 26.
2 Kwon, *Uncivil Youth*, 126.

3 Conner and Rosen, *Contemporary Youth Activism*; Kirshner, *Youth Activism*; Ginwright, Noguera, and Cammarota, *Beyond Resistance!*
4 Funders' Collaborative on Youth Organizing, *20 Years of Youth Power*.
5 Kirshner and Ginwright, "Youth Organizing"; Quinn and Nguyen, "Immigrant Youth Organizing"; Rogers and Terriquez, *Learning to Lead*.
6 During the 2019–20 academic year, only four of the forty-five students who regularly attended Teens Take Charge meetings were Asian American. The leadership team considered this pattern particularly problematic, due to a growing wave of opposition to changing selective admissions processes in immigrant Asian communities.
7 Rogers, Mediratta, and Shah, "Building Power, Learning Democracy"; Kirshner, "Power in Numbers"; Carey et al., "And School Won't Teach Me That!"; Gordon, *We Fight to Win*.
8 Taines, "Intervening in Alienation"; Carey et al., "And School Won't Teach Me That!"; Rosen, "So Much of My Very Soul"; Kirshner and Ginwright, "Youth Organizing."
9 Lee, White, and Dong, *Educating for Civic Reasoning and Discourse*, 97.
10 Rubin, "There's Still Not Justice."
11 Kirshner, *Youth Activism*, 51.
12 Schneider and Ingram, "Social Construction of Target Populations."
13 Phillippo, *Contest without Winners*; Ball et al., "Policy Actors."
14 Kwon, *Uncivil Youth*, 94.
15 Wells, Fox, and Cordova-Coba, *How Racially Diverse Schools*.
16 Phillippo, *Contest without Winners*; Rosen, "So Much of My Very Soul"; Ball et al., "Policy Actors."
17 Kwon, *Uncivil Youth*, 172.
18 Hagerman, *White Kids*.

CONCLUSION

1 Algar and Feis, "De Blasio Schools Boss."
2 Mays, Rubinstein, and Fitzsimmons, "A Train and the Macarena."
3 Carter and Merry, "Wall to Wall."
4 Noguera, *City Schools and the American Dream*, 17.
5 Anyon, *Radical Possibilities*, 177.
6 Douglass, "Significance of Emancipation in the West Indies."
7 Stockstill, *False Starts*, 155.
8 Carter and Merry, "Wall to Wall," 19.
9 McGhee, *Sum of Us*.
10 Tullis, "Brooklyn Middle School Integration Plan."
11 Shalaby, *Troublemakers*, 177.
12 Shalaby, 174.
13 Abu El-Haj and Rubin, "Realizing the Equity-Minded Aspirations."

14 Hammond, *Culturally Responsive Teaching*; Ladson-Billings, "Culturally Relevant Pedagogy 2.0"; Paris, "Culturally Sustaining Pedagogy."

APPENDIX

1 Freidus and Noguera, "From 'Good Will' to 'Anachronism.'"
2 Freidus, "Great School Benefits Us All."
3 Mehan, "Competent Student," 139.
4 Lewis, *Race in the Schoolyard*, 202.
5 Ferguson, *Bad Boys*; Thorne, *Gender Play*.
6 Lawrence-Lightfoot, "Reflections on Portraiture," 5.
7 Lawrence-Lightfoot and Davis, *Art and Science of Portraiture*.
8 Jerolmack and Murphy, "Ethical Dilemmas."

BIBLIOGRAPHY

Abu El-Haj, Thea Renda. *Elusive Justice: Wrestling with Difference and Educational Equity in Everyday Practice*. New York: Routledge, 2006.

Abu El-Haj, Thea Renda, and Beth C. Rubin. "Realizing the Equity-Minded Aspirations of Detracking and Inclusion: Toward a Capacity-Oriented Framework for Teacher Education." *Curriculum Inquiry* 39, no. 3 (June 2009): 435–63. https://doi.org/10.1111/j.1467-873X.2009.00451.x.

Algar, Selim, and Aaron Feis. "De Blasio Schools Boss Carranza Lauds 'Opportunity' of Deadly Coronavirus: 'Never Waste a Good Crisis.'" *New York Post*, May 5, 2020. https://nypost.com.

Allport, Gordon. *The Nature of Prejudice*. Cambridge, MA: Addison-Wesley, 1954.

Annamma, Subini Ancy. "Whiteness as Property: Innocence and Ability in Teacher Education." *Urban Review* 47, no. 2 (2015): 293–316. https://doi.org/10.1007/s11256-014-0293-6.

Anyon, Jean. *Ghetto Schooling*. New York: Teachers College Press, 1997.

———. *Radical Possibilities: Public Policy, Urban Education, and a New Social Movement*. New York: Routledge, 2005.

———. "Social Class and the Hidden Curriculum of Work." *Journal of Education* 162, no. 1 (1980): 67–92.

Au, Wayne. "Teaching under the New Taylorism: High-Stakes Testing and the Standardization of the 21st Century Curriculum." *Journal of Curriculum Studies* 43, no. 1 (February 2011): 25–45. https://doi.org/10.1080/00220272.2010.521261.

Baldridge, Bianca J. *Reclaiming Community: Race and the Uncertain Future of Youth Work*. Stanford, CA: Stanford University Press, 2019.

Ball, Stephen J., Meg Maguire, Annette Braun, and Kate Hoskins. "Policy Actors: Doing Policy Work in Schools." *Discourse* 32, no. 4 (2011): 625–39. https://doi.org/10.1080/01596306.2011.601565.

———. "Policy Subjects and Policy Actors in Schools: Some Necessary but Insufficient Analyses." *Discourse* 32, no. 4 (2011): 611–24. https://doi.org/10.1080/01596306.2011.601564.

Bell, Joyce M., and Douglas Hartmann. "Diversity in Everyday Discourse: Consequences of 'Happy Talk.'" *American Sociological Review* 72, no. 1997 (2007): 895–914.

Berrey, Ellen. *The Enigma of Diversity: The Language of Race and the Limits of Racial Justice*. Chicago: University of Chicago Press, 2015.

Bischoff, Kendra, and Laura Tach. "School Choice, Neighborhood Change, and Racial Imbalance between Public Elementary Schools and Surrounding Neighborhoods." *Sociological Science* 7 (2020): 75–99. https://doi.org/10.15195/v7.a4.

Bonastia, Christopher. *The Battle Nearer to Home: The Persistence of School Segregation in New York City.* Stanford, CA: Stanford University Press, 2022.

Brown-Saracino, Japonica. *A Neighborhood That Never Changes.* Chicago: University of Chicago Press, 2010.

Caraballo, Limarys. "Being 'Loud': Identities-in-Practice in a Figured World of Achievement." *American Educational Research Journal* 56, no. 4 (2019): 1281–1317. https://doi.org/10.3102/0002831218816059.

Carey, Roderick L., Thomas Akiva, Haya Abdellatif, and Kendell A. Daughtry. "'And School Won't Teach Me That!': Urban Youth Activism Programs as Transformative Sites for Critical Adolescent Learning." *Journal of Youth Studies* 24, no. 7 (2021): 941–60. https://doi.org/10.1080/13676261.2020.1784400.

Carter, Prudence L. *Stubborn Roots: Race, Culture, and Inequality in U.S. and South African Schools.* New York: Oxford University Press, 2012.

Carter, Prudence L., and Michael S. Merry. "Wall to Wall: Examining the Ecology of Racial and Educational Inequality with Research." White paper. Spencer Foundation, Chicago, December 2021.

Carter, Prudence L., and Kevin Welner. *Closing the Opportunity Gap: What America Must Do to Give Every Child an Even Chance.* New York: Oxford University Press, 2013.

Carter Andrews, Dorinda J., Tashal Brown, Eliana Castro, and Effat Id-Deen. "The Impossibility of Being 'Perfect and White': Black Girls' Racialized and Gendered Schooling Experiences." *American Educational Research Journal* 6, no. 6 (2019): 1–42. https://doi.org/10.3102/0002831219849392.

Castagno, Angelina E. *Educated in Whiteness: Good Intentions and Diversity in Schools.* Minneapolis: University of Minnesota Press, 2014.

Castillo, Elise. "A Neoliberal Grammar of Schooling? How a Progressive Charter School Moved toward Market Values." *American Journal of Education* 126 (August 2020): 519–47.

Cohen, Cathy J. *Democracy Remixed: Black Youth and the Future of American Politics.* New York: Oxford University Press, 2010.

Cohen, Danielle. *NYC School Segregation Report Card: Still Last, Action Needed Now.* Los Angeles: UCLA Civil Rights Project / Proyecto Derechos Civiles, 2021.

Cohen, David K., and Jal D. Mehta. "Why Reform Sometimes Succeeds: Understanding the Conditions That Produce Reforms That Last." *American Educational Research Journal* 54, no. 4 (2017): 644–90. https://doi.org/10.3102/0002831217700078.

Conner, Jerusha, and Sonia M. Rosen, eds. *Contemporary Youth Activism: Advancing Social Justice in the United States.* Santa Barbara, CA: Praeger, 2016.

Cordova-Cobo, Diana, and Ingrid Gould Ellen. *State of New York City's Housing and Neighborhoods: The Diversity of New York City's Neighborhoods and Schools.* New York: NYU Furman Center, 2018.

Crenshaw, Kimberlé. "Mapping the Margins: Intersectionality, Identity Politics, and Violence against Women of Color." *Stanford Law Review* 43, no. 6 (1991): 1241–99.

Cucchiara, Maia Bloomfield. *Marketing Schools, Marketing Cities: Who Wins and Who Loses When Schools Become Urban Amenities.* Chicago: University of Chicago Press, 2013.

Deliovsky, Kathy. "Normative White Femininity: Race, Gender and the Politics of Beauty." *Atlantis: Critical Studies in Gender, Culture & Social Justice* 33, no. 1 (2008): 49–59.

Delmont, Matthew F. *Why Busing Failed: Race, Media, and the National Resistance to School Desegregation.* Berkeley: University of California Press, 2016.

De Royston, Maxine McKinney, Carol Lee, Na'ilah Suad Nasir, and Roy Pea. "Rethinking Schools, Rethinking Learning." *Phi Delta Kappan* 102, no. 3 (November 2020): 8–13. https://doi.org/10.1177/0031721720970693.

Diamond, John B. "Defending the Color Line: White Supremacy and the Legacy of *Brown*." *Educational Researcher* 53, no. 3 (2024). https://doi.org/10.3102/0013189X231216450.

Diamond, John B., and Louis M. Gomez. "Disrupting White Supremacy and Anti-Black Racism in Educational Organizations." *Educational Researcher*, March 29, 2023. https://doi.org/10.3102/0013189X231161054.

Diamond, John B., and Amanda E. Lewis. "Opportunity Hoarding and the Maintenance of 'White' Educational Space." *American Behavioral Scientist* 66, no. 11 (2022). https://doi.org/10.1177/00027642211066048.

———. "Race and Discipline at a Racially Mixed Suburban High School: Status, Capital, and the Practice of Organizational Routines." *Peabody Journal of Education*, 2016. https://doi.org/10.1080/0161956X.2016.1184951.

Dobbs, Jennifer, David H. Arnold, and Greta L. Doctoroff. "Attention in the Preschool Classroom: The Relationships among Child Gender, Child Misbehavior, and Types of Teacher Attention." *Early Child Development and Care* 174, no. 3 (2004): 281–95. https://doi.org/10.1080/0300443032000153598.

Douglass, Frederick. "The Significance of Emancipation in the West Indies: An Address Delivered in Canandaigua, New York, on August 3, 1857." Frederick Douglass Papers. https://frederickdouglasspapersproject.com.

Du Bois, W. E. B. "Does the Negro Need Separate Schools?" *Journal of Negro Education* 4, no. 3 (1935): 328–35. https://doi.org/10.2307/2291871.

Dumas, Michael J. "Against the Dark: Antiblackness in Education Policy and Discourse." *Theory into Practice* 55, no. 1 (2016): 11–19. https://doi.org/10.1080/00405841.2016.1116852.

———. "Beginning and Ending with Black Suffering: A Meditation on and against Racial Justice in Education." In *Toward What Justice? Describing Diverse Dreams of Justice in Education*, edited by Eve Tuck and K. Wayne Yang, 29–46. New York: Routledge, 2018.

Elliott, Sinikka, and Sarah Bowen. "Defending Motherhood: Morality, Responsibility, and Double Binds in Feeding Children." *Journal of Marriage and Family* 80, no. 2 (2018): 499–520. https://doi.org/10.1111/jomf.12465.

Elwert, Felix, Tamás Keller, and Andreas Kotsadam. "Rearranging the Desk Chairs: A Large Randomized Field Experiment on the Effects of Close Contact on Interethnic Relations." *American Journal of Sociology* 128, no. 6 (May 1, 2023): 1809–40. https://doi.org/10.1086/724865.

Epstein, Rebecca, Jamilia J. Blake, and Thalia González. *Girlhood Interrupted: The Erasure of Black Girls' Childhood*. Washington, DC: Georgetown Center on Poverty and Inequality, 2017.

Erden, Feyza, and Charles H. Wolfgang. "An Exploration of the Differences in Prekindergarten, Kindergarten, and First Grade Teachers' Beliefs Related to Discipline When Dealing with Male and Female Students." *Early Child Development and Care* 174, no. 1 (2004): 3–11. https://doi.org/10.1080/0300443032000103098.

Evans, Shani Adia. "'I Wanted Diversity, but Not So Much': Middle-Class White Parents, School Choice, and the Persistence of Anti-Black Stereotypes." *Urban Education* 59, no. 3 (2021): 911–40. https://doi.org/10.1177/00420859211031952.

Ewing, Eve L. *Ghosts in the Schoolyard: Racism and School Closings on Chicago's South Side*. Chicago: University of Chicago Press, 2018.

Ferguson, Ann Arnett. *Bad Boys: Public Schools in the Making of Black Masculinity*. Ann Arbor: University of Michigan Press, 2000.

Fine, Michelle, Lois Weis, and Linda C. Powell. "Communities of Difference: A Critical Look at Desegregated Spaces Created for and by Youth." *Harvard Educational Review* 67, no. 2 (1997): 247–84.

Fish, Rachel Elizabeth. "The Racialized Construction of Exceptionality: Experimental Evidence of Race/Ethnicity Effects on Teachers' Interventions." *Social Science Research* 62 (2017): 317–34. https://doi.org/10.1016/j.ssresearch.2016.08.007.

Frankenberg, Erica, and Gary Orfield. *Lessons in Integration: Realizing the Promise of Racial Diversity in American Schools*. Charlottesville: University of Virginia Press, 2007.

Freidus, Alexandra. "'A Great School Benefits Us All': Advantaged Parents and the Gentrification of an Urban Public School." *Urban Education* 54, no. 8 (2019): 1–28. https://doi.org/10.1177/0042085916636656.

———. "'I Didn't Have a Lesson': Politics and Pedagogy in a Diversifying Middle School." *Teachers College Record* 122, no. 7 (2020): 1–40.

———. "Modes of Belonging: Debating School Demographics in Gentrifying New York." *American Educational Research Journal* 57, no. 2 (2020): 808–39. https://doi.org/10.3102/0002831219863372.

———. "'Problem Children' and 'Children with Problems': Discipline and Innocence in a Gentrifying Elementary School." *Harvard Educational Review* 90, no. 4 (2020): 550–73. https://doi.org/10.17763/1943-5045-90.4.550.

Freidus, Alexandra, and Pedro A. Noguera. "From 'Good Will' to 'Anachronism': Racial Discourse, Shifting Demographics, and the Role of School Desegregation in the Public Good." *Humanity & Society* 39, no. 4 (2015): 394–418. https://doi.org/10.1177/0160597615601716.

Funders' Collaborative on Youth Organizing. *20 Years of Youth Power: The 2020 National Youth Organizing Field Scan*. New York: Funders' Collaborative on Youth Organizing, 2020.

Gill, Lauren. "Farina: How PR and Power Brunches with Developers Can Desegregate Schools." *Brooklyn Paper*, May 4, 2016. www.brooklynpaper.com.

Gilliam, Walter S., Angela N. Maupin, Chin R. Reyes, Maria Accavitti, and Frederick Shic. "Do Early Educators' Implicit Biases Regarding Sex and Race Relate to Behavior Expectations and Recommendations of Preschool Expulsions and Suspensions?" Research study brief. Yale University Child Study Center, New Haven, CT, 2016.

Ginwright, Shawn, Pedro A. Noguera, and Julio Cammarota. *Beyond Resistance! Youth Activism and Community Change: New Democratic Possibilities for Practice and Policy for America's Youth*. New York: Routledge, 2006.

Goff, Phillip Atiba, Matthew Christian Jackson, Brooke Allison Lewis Di Leone, Carmen Marie Culotta, and Natalie Ann DiTomasso. "The Essence of Innocence: Consequences of Dehumanizing Black Children." *Journal of Personality and Social Psychology* 106, no. 4 (2014): 526–45. https://doi.org/10.1037/a0035663.

Gordon, Hava R. *This Is Our School! Race and Community Resistance to School Reform*. New York: New York University Press, 2021.

———. *We Fight to Win: Inequality and the Politics of Youth Activism*. New Brunswick, NJ: Rutgers University Press, 2010.

Gregory, Anne, Russell J. Skiba, and Pedro A. Noguera. "The Achievement Gap and the Discipline Gap: Two Sides of the Same Coin?" *Educational Researcher* 39, no. 1 (2010): 59–68. https://doi.org/10.3102/0013189X09357621.

Hagerman, Margaret A. "Racial Ideology and White Youth: From Middle Childhood to Adolescence." *Sociology of Race and Ethnicity* 6, no. 3 (2020): 319–32. https://doi.org/10.1177/2332649219853309.

———. *White Kids: Growing Up with Privilege in a Racially Divided America*. New York: New York University Press, 2018.

Hammond, Zaretta L. *Culturally Responsive Teaching and the Brain: Promoting Authentic Engagement and Rigor among Culturally and Linguistically Diverse Students*. Thousand Oaks, CA: Corwin, 2015.

Harris, Cheryl I. "Whiteness as Property." *Harvard Law Review* 106, no. 8 (1993): 1707–91.

Hatt, Beth. "Smartness as a Cultural Practice in Schools." *American Educational Research Journal* 49, no. 3 (2012): 438–60. https://doi.org/10.3102/0002831211415661.

Hemphill, Clara, and Nicole Mader. *Segregated Schools in Integrated Neighborhoods: The City's Schools Are Even More Divided than Our Housing*. New York: New School Center for New York City Affairs, 2016.

Holloway, Jessica, and Jory Brass. "Making Accountable Teachers: The Terrors and Pleasures of Performativity." *Journal of Education Policy* 33, no. 3 (May 4, 2018): 361–82. https://doi.org/10.1080/02680939.2017.1372636.

Horsford, Sonya Douglass. *Learning in a Burning House: Educational Inequality, Ideology, and (Dis)Integration.* New York: Teachers College Press, 2011.

Irby, Decoteau J. *Stuck Improving: Racial Equity and School Leadership.* Cambridge, MA: Harvard Education Press, 2021.

Jackson, Philip. *Life in Classrooms.* New York: Holt, Rinehart and Winston, 1968.

Jerolmack, Colin, and Alexandra K. Murphy. "The Ethical Dilemmas and Social Scientific Trade-Offs of Masking in Ethnography." *Sociological Methods and Research* 48, no. 4 (2019): 801–27. https://doi.org/10.1177/0049124117701483.

Johnson, Rucker C. *Children of the Dream: Why School Integration Works.* New York: Basic Books, 2019.

Kahlenberg, Richard D. *All Together Now: The Case for Economic Integration of the Public Schools.* Washington, DC: Brookings Institution Press, 2001.

Kao, Grace, and Kara Joyner. "Do Race and Ethnicity Matter among Friends? Activities among Interracial, Interethnic, and Intraethnic Adolescent Friends." *Sociological Quarterly* 45, no. 3 (2004): 557–73. https://doi.org/10.1111/j.1533-8525.2004.tb02303.x.

Kendi, Ibram. *How to Be an Antiracist.* New York: One World, 2019.

Kirshner, Ben. "'Power in Numbers': Youth Organizing as a Context for Exploring Civic Identity." *Journal of Research on Adolescence* 19, no. 3 (2009): 414–40. https://doi.org/10.1111/j.1532-7795.2009.00601.x.

———. *Youth Activism in an Era of Education Inequality.* New York: New York University Press, 2015.

Kirshner, Ben, and Shawn Ginwright. "Youth Organizing as a Developmental Context for African American and Latino Adolescents." *Child Development Perspectives* 6, no. 3 (2012): 288–94. https://doi.org/10.1111/j.1750-8606.2012.00243.x.

Kucsera, John, and Gary Orfield. *New York State's Extreme School Segregation: Inequality, Inaction and a Damaged Future.* Los Angeles: Civil Rights Project / Proyecto Derechos Civiles, 2014.

Kwon, Soo Ah. *Uncivil Youth: Race, Activism, and Affirmative Governmentality.* Durham, NC: Duke University Press, 2013.

Labaree, David F. "The Dynamic Tension at the Core of the Grammar of Schooling." *Phi Delta Kappan* 103, no. 2 (2021): 28–32. https://doi.org/10.1177/00317217211051141.

Ladson-Billings, Gloria. "Culturally Relevant Pedagogy 2.0: A.k.a. the Remix." *Harvard Educational Review* 84, no. 1 (2014): 74–84. https://doi.org/10.17763/haer.84.1.p2rj131485484751.

———. "From the Achievement Gap to the Education Debt: Understanding Achievement in U.S. Schools." *Educational Researcher* 35, no. 7 (2006): 3–12. https://doi.org/10.3102/0013189X035007003.

———. "Landing on the Wrong Note: The Price We Paid for *Brown.*" *Educational Researcher* 33, no. 7 (2004): 3–13. https://doi.org/10.3102/0013189X033007003.

———. "Toward a Theory of Culturally Relevant Pedagogy." *American Educational Research Journal* 32, no. 3 (1995): 465–91. https://doi.org/10.3102/00028312032003465.

Lareau, Annette. *Unequal Childhoods: Class, Race, and Family Life*. Berkeley: University of California Press, 2011.

Lawrence-Lightfoot, Sara. "Reflections on Portraiture: A Dialogue between Art and Science." *Qualitative Inquiry* 11, no. 1 (2005): 3–15. https://doi.org/10.1177/1077800404270955.

Lawrence-Lightfoot, Sara, and Jessica Hoffman Davis. *The Art and Science of Portraiture*. San Francisco: Jossey-Bass, 1997.

Lee, Carol D., Gregory White, and Dian Dong. *Educating for Civic Reasoning and Discourse*. Washington, DC: National Academy of Education, 2021.

Lewis, Amanda E. *Race in the Schoolyard: Negotiating the Color Line in Classrooms and Communities*. New Brunswick, NJ: Rutgers University Press, 2003.

Lewis, Amanda E., and John B. Diamond. *Despite the Best Intentions: How Racial Inequality Thrives in Good Schools*. New York: Oxford University Press, 2015.

Lipman, Pauline. "The Cultural Politics of Mixed-Income Schools and Housing: A Racialized Discourse of Displacement, Exclusion, and Control." *Anthropology & Education Quarterly* 40, no. 3 (September 2009): 215–36. https://doi.org/10.1111/j.1548-1492.2009.01042.x.

———. *High Stakes Education: Inequality, Globalization, and Urban School Reform*. New York: RoutledgeFalmer, 2004.

———. *The New Political Economy of Urban Education: Neoliberalism, Race, and the Right to the City*. New York: Routledge, 2011.

MacLure, Maggie, Liz Jones, Rachel Holmes, and Christina Macrae. "Becoming a Problem: Behaviour and Reputation in the Early Years Classroom." *British Educational Research Journal* 3, no. 3 (2012): 447–71. https://doi.org/10.1080/01411926.2011.552709.

Mader, Nicole, Clara Hemphill, and Qasim Abbas. *The Paradox of Choice: How School Choice Divides New York City Elementary School*. New York: New School Center for New York City Affairs, 2018.

Mays, Jeffery C., Dana Rubinstein, and Emma G. Fitzsimmons. "The A Train and the Macarena: 5 Highlights from the Mayor's Race." *New York Times*, March 8, 2021. www.nytimes.com.

McDermott, Ray. "The Acquisition of a Child by a Learning Disability." In *Understanding Practice: Perspectives on Activity and Context*, edited by Seth Chaiklin and Jean Lave, 269–305. Cambridge: Cambridge University Press, 1993.

McGhee, Chy, and Gary Anderson. "Gentrification, Market Regimes, and the New Entrepreneurial Principal: Enacting Integration or Displacement?" *Leadership and Policy in Schools* 18, no. 2 (2019): 180–94. https://doi.org/10.1080/15700763.2019.1611871.

McGhee, Heather. *The Sum of Us: What Racism Costs Everyone and How We Can Prosper Together*. New York: One World, 2021.

Meckler, Laura. "NYC's Black Schools Chief Isn't Sure Racial Integration Is the Answer." *Washington Post*, November 17, 2022. www.washingtonpost.com.

Mehan, Hugh. "The Competent Student." *Anthropology & Education Quarterly* 11, no. 3 (1980): 131–52. https://doi.org/10.1525/aeq.1980.11.3.05x1865s.

———. "Understanding Inequality in Schools: The Contribution of Interpretive Studies." *Sociology of Education* 65, no. 1 (1992): 1–20. https://doi.org/10.2307/2112689.

Mehta, Jal. "Possible Futures: Toward a New Grammar of Schooling." *Phi Delta Kappan*, January 24, 2022. https://kappanonline.org.

Mehta, Jal, and Amanda Datnow. "Changing the Grammar of Schooling: An Appraisal and a Research Agenda." *American Journal of Education* 126, no. 4 (2020): 491–98. https://doi.org/10.1086/709960.

Meier, Kenneth J., Joseph Stewart, and Robert E. England. *Race, Class, and Education: The Politics of Second Generation Discrimination*. Madison: University of Wisconsin Press, 1989.

Melamed, Jodi. "The Spirit of Neoliberalism: From Racial Liberalism to Neoliberal Multiculturalism." *Social Text* 24, no. 4 (89) (December 1, 2006): 1–24. https://doi.org/10.1215/01642472-2006-009.

Menken, Kate, Ivana Espinet, and Sharon Avni. "'There Was Nothing Here': School Leaders Using Dual Language Bilingual Education Programs as a Formula to Re-engineer Student Populations for School Turnaround." *Educational Policy*, 38, no. 2 (2024): 448–78. https://doi.org/10.1177/08959048231159919.

Metz, Mary Haywood. "Real School: A Universal Drama amid Disparate Experience." *Journal of Education Policy* 4, no. 5 (1989): 75–91. https://doi.org/10.1080/0268093890040505.

Mordechay, Kfir, and Jennifer Ayscue. *School Integration in Gentrifying Neighborhoods: Evidence from New York City*. Los Angeles: Civil Rights Project / Proyecto Derechos Civiles, 2019.

———. *White Growth, Persistent Segregation: Could Gentrification Become Integration?* Los Angeles: Civil Rights Project / Proyecto Derechos Civiles, 2017.

Morris, Edward W. "'Ladies' or 'Loudies'? Perceptions and Experiences of Black Girls in Classrooms." *Youth and Society* 38, no. 4 (2007): 490–515. https://doi.org/10.1177/0044118X06296778.

Musto, Michela. "Brilliant or Bad: The Gendered Social Construction of Exceptionalism in Early Adolescence." *American Sociological Review* 84, no. 3 (2019): 369–93. https://doi.org/10.1177/0003122419837567.

Nasir, Na'ilah Suad, Carol D. Lee, Roy Pea, and Maxine McKinney de Royston. "Rethinking Learning: What the Interdisciplinary Science Tells Us." *Educational Researcher* 50, no. 8 (2021): 557–65. https://doi.org/10.3102/0013189X211047251.

Nelson, Joseph Derrick. "Relationships of (Re)Imagining: Black Boyhood, the Race-Gender Discipline Gap, and Early-Childhood Teacher Education." *New Educator* 16, no. 2 (2020): 122–30. https://doi.org/10.1080/1547688X.2020.1739932.

New York City Department of Education. "Diversity in Our Schools." Accessed July 23, 2024. www.schools.nyc.gov.

New York State Education Department. "2015–18 Title I School Improvement Section 1003(a) Socioeconomic Integration Pilot Program." Grant information document, Albany NY, 2014. www.p12.nysed.gov.

Noguera, Pedro A. *City Schools and the American Dream*. New York: Teachers College Press, 2003.

———. *The Trouble with Black Boys, and Other Reflections on Race, Equity, and the Future of Public Education*. San Francisco: Jossey-Bass, 2008.

Noguera, Pedro A., and Esa Syeed. *City Schools and the American Dream 2: The Enduring Promise of Public Education*. New York: Teachers College Press, 2020.

Noguera, Pedro A., and Jean Yonemura Wing. *Unfinished Business: Closing the Racial Achievement Gap in Our Schools*. San Francisco: Jossey-Bass, 2006.

Nygreen, Kysa. *These Kids: Identity, Agency, and Social Justice at a Last Chance High School*. Chicago: University of Chicago Press, 2013.

Oakes, Jeannie. *Keeping Track: How Schools Structure Inequality*. New Haven, CT: Yale University Press, 2005.

Ochoa, Gilda L. *Academic Profiling: Latinos, Asian Americans, and the Achievement Gap*. Minneapolis: University of Minnesota Press, 2013.

Omi, Michael, and Howard Winant. *Racial Formation in the United States: From the 1960s to the 1990s*. New York: Routledge, 1994.

Orfield, Gary. Foreword to *New York State's Extreme School Segregation: Inequality, Inaction and a Damaged Future*, by John Kucsera and Gary Orfield, iii–v. Los Angeles: Civil Rights Project / Proyecto Derechos Civiles, 2014.

———. Foreword to *NYC School Segregation Report Card: Still Last, Action Needed Now*, by Danielle Cohen, 1–8. Los Angeles: UCLA Civil Rights Project / Proyecto Derechos Civiles, 2021.

Orfield, Gary, and Erica Frankenberg and Associates. *Educational Delusions? Why Choice Can Deepen Inequality and How to Make Schools Fair*. Berkeley: University of California Press, 2013.

Owens, Jayanti. "Double Jeopardy: Teacher Biases, Racialized Organizations, and the Production of Racial/Ethnic Disparities in School Discipline." *American Sociological Review* 87, no. 6 (December 2022): 1007–48. https://doi.org/10.1177/00031224221135810.

Paris, Django. "Culturally Sustaining Pedagogy: A Needed Change in Stance, Terminology, and Practice." *Educational Researcher* 41, no. 3 (2012): 93–97. https://doi.org/10.3102/0013189X12441244.

Paris, Django, and H. Samy Alim. "What Are We Seeking to Sustain through Culturally Sustaining Pedagogy? A Loving Critique Forward." *Harvard Educational Review* 84, no. 1 (2014): 85–101.

Pascoe, C. J. *Nice Is Not Enough: Inequality and the Limits of Kindness at American High School*. Berkeley: University of California Press, 2023.

Pattillo, Mary. *Black on the Block: The Politics of Race and Class in the City*. Chicago: University of Chicago Press, 2007.
Pawlewicz, Diana D Amico. "Teacher Blame as the Grammar of Public School Reform." *History of Education Quarterly* 62, special issue 3 (2022): 291–311. https://doi.org/10.1017/heq.2022.16.
Phillippo, Kate. *A Contest without Winners: How Students Experience Competitive School Choice*. Minneapolis: University of Minnesota Press, 2019.
Pica-Smith, Cinzia. "Children Speak about Interethnic and Interracial Friendships in the Classroom Lessons for Teachers." *Multicultural Education* 17, no. 1 (2009): 38–47.
Pierce, Jill C. "Official Approaches to Equity and Democracy in New York City's School Closure, Consolidation, and Charter Co-Location Decisions." PhD diss., New York University, 2018.
Pollock, Mica. *Colormute: Race Talk Dilemmas in an American School*. Princeton, NJ: Princeton University Press, 2005.
———, ed. *Everyday Antiracism: Getting Real about Race in School*. New York: New Press, 2008.
Posey-Maddox, Linn. *When Middle-Class Parents Choose Urban Schools: Class, Race, and the Challenges of Equity in Public Education*. Chicago: University of Chicago Press, 2014.
Posey-Maddox, Linn, Maxine McKinney de Royston, Alea R. Holman, Raquel M. Rall, and Rachel Johnson. "Black Parents' Educational Decision-Making in Their Search for a 'Good' School." *Harvard Educational Review* 91, no. 1 (2021): 38–62.
powell, john a. "A New Theory of Integrated Education: True Integration." In *School Resegregation: Must the South Turn Back?*, edited by Gary Orfield and John Charles Boger, 281–304. Chapel Hill: University of North Carolina Press, 2009.
Quarles, Bradley, and Alisha Butler. "Toward a Multivocal Research Agenda on School Gentrification: A Critical Review of Current Literature." *Peabody Journal of Education* 93, no. 4 (2018): 1–15. https://doi.org/10.1080/0161956X.2018.1488399.
Quinn, Rand, and Chi Nguyen. "Immigrant Youth Organizing as Civic Preparation." *American Educational Research Journal* 54, no. 5 (2017): 972–1005. https://doi.org/10.3102/0002831217712946.
Ramey, David M. "The Social Structure of Criminalized and Medicalized School Discipline." *Sociology of Education* 88, no. 3 (2015): 181–201. https://doi.org/10.1177/0038040715587114.
Ray, Ranita. "Race-Conscious Racism: Alibis for Racial Harm in the Classroom." *Social Problems* 70, no. 3 (2023): 682–97. https://doi.org/10.1093/socpro/spac009.
———. "School as a Hostile Institution: How Black and Immigrant Girls of Color Experience the Classroom." *Gender and Society* 36, no. 1 (2022): 88–111. https://doi.org/10.1177/08912432211057916.
Ray, Victor. "A Theory of Racialized Organizations." *American Sociological Review* 84, no. 1 (2019): 26–53. https://doi.org/10.1177/0003122418822335.

Ridgeway, Cecilia L. "Framed before We Know It: How Gender Shapes Social Relations." *Gender & Society* 23, no. 2 (April 2009): 145–60. https://doi.org/10.1177/0891243208330313.

Rivera-McCutchen, Rosa L. *Radical Care: Leading for Justice in Urban Schools*. New York: Teachers College Press, 2021.

Roda, Allison, and Amy Stuart Wells. "School Choice Policies and Racial Segregation: Where White Parents' Good Intentions, Anxiety, and Privilege Collide." *American Journal of Education* 119, no. 2 (February 2013): 261–93. https://doi.org/10.1086/668753.

Rogers, John, Kavitha Mediratta, and Seema Shah. "Building Power, Learning Democracy." *Review of Research in Education* 36, no. 1 (2012): 43–66. https://doi.org/10.3102/0091732x11422328.

Rogers, John, and Veronica Terriquez. *Learning to Lead: The Impact of Youth Organizing on the Educational and Civic Trajectories of Low-Income Youth*. Los Angeles: Institute for Democracy, Education, and Access (IDEA) for the Charles Stewart Mott Foundation, 2013.

Rosen, Sonia M. "'So Much of My Very Soul': How Youth Organizers' Identity Projects Pave Agentive Pathways for Civic Engagement." *American Educational Research Journal* 56, no. 3 (2019): 1033–63. https://doi.org/10.3102/0002831218812028.

ross, kihana miraya. "Black Space in Education: Fugitive Resistance in the Afterlife of School Segregation." In *The Future Is Black: Afropessimism, Fugitivity, and Radical Hope in Education*, edited by Carl A. Grant, Ashley Woodson, and Michael J. Dumas, 47–54. New York: Routledge, 2021.

———. *On the Road to* Brown *and Beyond: Troubling Integration, Desegregation, and Segregation in the Fight for Black Educational Equity, Opportunity, and Justice*. Chicago: Spencer Foundation, 2021.

Royal, Camika, and Simone Gibson. "They Schools: Culturally Relevant Pedagogy under Siege." *Teachers College Record* 119 (January 2017): 1–25.

Rubin, Beth C. "'There's Still Not Justice': Youth Civic Identity Development amid Distinct School and Community Contexts." *Teachers College Record* 109, no. 2 (2007): 449–81.

Russo, Melissa. "Upper West Side School Rezoning Proposal Riles Parents." *NBC New York*, August 21, 2016. www.nbcnewyork.com.

Sattin-Bajaj, Carolyn, and Allison Roda. "Opportunity Hoarding in School Choice Contexts: The Role of Policy Design in Promoting Middle-Class Parents' Exclusionary Behaviors." *Educational Policy* 34, no. 7 (2020): 1–44. https://doi.org/10.1177/0895904818802106.

Schneider, Anne, and Helen Ingram. "Social Construction of Target Populations: Implications for Politics and Policy." *American Political Science Review* 87, no. 2 (1993): 334–47.

Schneider, Jack, Peter Piazza, Rachel S. White, and Ashley Carey. "Student Experience Outcomes in Racially Integrated Schools: Looking Beyond Test Scores in

Six Districts." *Education and Urban Society* 54, no. 3 (2022): 330–60. https://doi.org/10.1177/00131245211004569.

School Diversity Advisory Group. *Making the Grade: The Path to Real Integration and Equity for NYC Public School Students*. New York City: School Diversity Advisory Group, 2019.

Shalaby, Carla. *Troublemakers: Lessons in Freedom from Young Children in School*. New York: New Press, 2017.

Shange, Savannah. *Progressive Dystopia: Abolition, Antiblackness, and Schooling in San Francisco*. Durham, NC: Duke University Press, 2019.

Siddle-Walker, Vanessa. *Their Highest Potential: An African American School Community in the Segregated South*. Chapel Hill: University of North Carolina Press, 1996.

Sojoyner, Damien M. *First Strike: Educational Enclosures in Black Los Angeles*. Minneapolis: University of Minnesota Press, 2016.

Solórzano, Daniel G., and Tara J. Yosso. "Critical Race Methodology: Counter Storytelling as an Analytical Framework for Education Research." *Qualitative Inquiry* 8, no. 1 (2002): 23–44. https://doi.org/10.1177/107780040200800103.

Starck, Jordan G., Travis Riddle, Stacey Sinclair, and Natasha Warikoo. "Teachers Are People Too: Examining the Racial Bias of Teachers Compared to Other American Adults." *Educational Researcher* 49, no. 4 (May 2020): 273–84. https://doi.org/10.3102/0013189X20912758.

Stockstill, Casey. *False Starts: The Segregated Lives of Preschoolers*. Critical Perspectives on Youth. New York: New York University Press, 2023.

Syeed, Esa. "There Goes the PTA: Building Parent Identity, Relationships, and Power in Gentrifying Schools." *Equity & Excellence in Education* 51, nos. 3–4 (2018): 284–300. https://doi.org/10.1080/10665684.2018.1563875.

Taines, Cynthia. "Intervening in Alienation: The Outcomes for Urban Youth of Participating in School Activism." *American Educational Research Journal* 49, no. 1 (2012): 53–86. https://doi.org/10.3102/0002831211411079.

Tatum, Beverly Daniel. *Why Are All the Black Kids Sitting Together in the Cafeteria? And Other Conversations about Race*. New York: Basic Books, 2017.a

Tenenbaum, Harriet R., and Martin D. Ruck. "Are Teachers' Expectations Different for Racial Minority than for European American Students? A Meta-analysis." *Journal of Educational Psychology* 99, no. 2 (May 2007): 253–73. https://doi.org/10.1037/0022-0663.99.2.253.

Theoharris, Jeanne. *A More Beautiful and Terrible History: The Uses and Misuses of Civil Rights History*. Boston: Beacon, 2018.

Thorne, Barrie. *Gender Play: Girls and Boys in School*. New Brunswick, NJ: Rutgers University Press, 1993.

Tullis, Tracy. "A Brooklyn Middle School Integration Plan Shows Some Patterns Are Hard to Break." *Chalkbeat New York*, November 14, 2022. www.chalkbeat.org.

Turner, Erica O. "Marketing Diversity: Selling School Districts in a Racialized Marketplace." *Journal of Education Policy* 33, no. 6 (2018): 793–817. https://doi.org/10.1080/02680939.2017.1386327.

———. *Suddenly Diverse: How School Districts Manage Race and Inequality*. Chicago: University of Chicago Press, 2020.

Tyack, David, and Larry Cuban. *Tinkering toward Utopia: A Century of Public School Reform*. Cambridge, MA: Harvard University Press, 1995.

Tyack, David, and William Tobin. "The 'Grammar' of Schooling: Why Has It Been so Hard to Change?" *American Educational Research Journal* 31, no. 3 (1994): 453–79. https://doi.org/10.3102/00028312031003453.

Tyson, Karolyn. *Integration Interrupted: Tracking, Black Students, and Acting White after Brown*. New York: Oxford University Press, 2011.

Valenzuela, Angela. *Subtractive Schooling: U.S.-Mexican Youth and the Politics of Caring*. Albany: State University of New York Press, 1999.

Veiga, Christina. "Chancellor Richard Carranza Stands by His Tweet of Viral Video in Upper West Side Integration Fight." *Chalkbeat New York*, April 27, 2018. www.chalkbeat.org.

Wall, Patrick. "De Blasio: City Must Respect Families' Investments amid School Diversity Debates." *Chalkbeat New York*, November 6, 2015. www.chalkbeat.org.

Weis, Lois, and Michelle Fine. "Critical Bifocality and Circuits of Privilege: Expanding Critical Ethnographic Theory and Design." *Harvard Educational Review* 82, no. 2 (2012): 173–201.

Wells, Amy Stuart. "The Process of Racial Resegregation in Housing and Schools: The Sociology of Reputation." In *Emerging Trends in the Social and Behavioral Sciences*, edited by Robert A. Scott and Marlis C. Buchmann, 1–14. New York: Wiley, 2018.

Wells, Amy Stuart, Lauren Fox, and Diana Cordova-Coba. *How Racially Diverse Schools and Classrooms Can Benefit All Students*. Washington, DC: Century Foundation, 2016.

Wells, Amy Stuart, Jennifer Jellison Holme, Anita Tijerina Revilla, and Awo Korantemaa Atanda. *Both Sides Now: The Story of School Desegregation's Graduates*. Berkeley: University of California Press, 2009.

Wortham, Stanton. *Learning Identity: The Joint Emergence of Social Identification and Academic Learning*. New York: Cambridge University Press, 2006.

Zimmer, Amy, and Noah Hurowitz. "Schools Boss Touts Pen Pal System as Substitute for Racial Integration." *DNA Info*, October 29, 2015. www.dnainfo.com.

Zimmerman, Alex. "Fariña to Parents: We Need 'Organic' Plans, Not Mandates, to Diversify Schools." *Chalkbeat*, February 24, 2016. www.chalkbeat.org.

Zimmermann, Calvin Rashaud. "The Penalty of Being a Young Black Girl: Kindergarten Teachers' Perceptions of Children's Problem Behaviors and Student-Teacher Conflict by the Intersection of Race and Gender." *Journal of Negro Education* 87, no. 2 (2018): 154–68. https://doi.org/10.7709/jnegroeducation.87.2.0154.

INDEX

Page numbers in *italics* indicate photos.

Abu El-Haj, Thea, 101
academic ability, 99
academic skills, 121
accountability reforms, 97; Bloomberg-era, 24; market-based, 85, 149, 157; standardized test scores and, 94
activism, parent, 8. *See also* youth organization
Adams, Eric, 142
Adara (student), 126–27
ADHD. *See* attention deficit hyperactivity disorder
admissions, priority groups for, 28
adult identities, 163
advocacy: diversity, 19; grassroots, 142; for integration, 141, 159; political, 109–10; redistributing of resources and, 6; for school segregation, 9, 21; skills, 139; by youth activists, 113
affirmative action, 6
Aida (student), 69
Ali, Sami, 101
Allport, Gordon, 72
Amina (student), 115–18, 128
ancient civilizations, 93
ancient Egyptian caste system, 94
Ancient Greece, 87
Annie (staff member), 34, 37–38
Anthony (youth leader), 124
antiblackness, 6, 105; diversity and, 91; education research and, 82, 104; grammar, 102–4

antiracism, 91, 147; demographics as, 79; of M.S. 917, 78–81; Myers and, 12–13, 78; official, 27; as verb, 12–13
anxiety, 57–59
Anyon, Jean, 144
Apple, Ms. (teacher), 76–77, 95, 102
Arab American students, 78
Arnett (Superintendent), 16–17, 19, 21, 31–37, 158, 161
Asian American students, 5–6, 122, 127; in District 41, 32; in TTC, 175n6 (chap. 4); "urban schools" demographics and, 7
attention deficit hyperactivity disorder (ADHD), 64

backlash, White, 30
Bacon's Rebellion, 92
"bad choices," 55
Baker, Ella, 8–9
Baldridge, Bianca, 108
Ball, Stephen, 10, 137
Banks, David, 1, 13, 142, 144
Bedford-Stuyvesant, New York, 24
Bell, Joyce, 25
Berkeley High School, 2
Berrey, Ellen, 25, 34, 43, 60
best practices, 104
bias, racial, 12, 72
bilingual classrooms, dual-language, 33
birth rates, decreased, 142
Black boys, 53
Black girls, 53

191

Black History Month, 91, 95–96, 100, 103–4
Black Lives Matter, 78
"Black National Anthem" ("Lift Ev'ry Voice and Sing"), 91
Black students, 3, 83, 117, 122, 131, 133, 161–62; in District 41, 32; good grades for, 98–102; grammar of school and, 82; hidden curriculum of diversity and, 4–7; low-income, 2, 20, 28, 30–33, 39, 43, 49; at M.S. 917, 78–80; perceptions of, 51; public housing for, 15; "urban schools" demographics and, 7
Black Student Union, 124
Blake (Principal), 16–17, 31, 35–37, 40–41, 50, 67–69, 80, 161
de Blasio, Bill, 23–24, 26, 35, 141, 165
Bloomberg, Michael, 20, 23–24, 26, 142, 157
boycotts, 8, 119
boys, Black, 53
Brass, Jory, 97
Brooklyn, New York, 1, 8, 24
Brown students, 117
Brown v. Board of Education, 4, 6, 8, 11, 26, 43, 83, 112
Bush, George W., 20
busing, 26, 30

Carranza, Richard, 1, 112, 125, 141–42
Carter, Prudence, 72, 90–91, 94, 148
caste system, ancient Egyptian, 94
Castillo, Elise, 85
catchment zone, 15
CEC. *See* Community Education Council
Chalkbeat (podcast), 159
change, social, 122
childhood, middle, 103
choice-based enrollment, 22
circuits of dispossession and privilege, 10
civil discourse, 122

civilizations, ancient, 93
Civil Rights Act (1964), 8–9
civil rights movement, 91, 119
Civil Rights Project (UCLA), 9, 21–22, 31
civil skills, 113–14
Clark, Kenneth, 8
classroom learning, 55, 82, 87–88, 93–96
classroom norms, 43, 63, 100–101
Cohen, Cathy, 20
collective labor, 135
communal activity, schooling as, 84
community-based organizations, 137–38
Community Education Council (CEC), 15, 123, 158
community partnership, 66
community school districts, 20
compliance, 76
constraints, 103
"core academic classes," 96
COVID-19 pandemic, 116, 119, 136–37, 141–42
critical race theory, 9
cross-racial friendships, 90
CRP. *See* culturally relevant pedagogy
Cuban, Larry, 81
Cucchiara, Maia, 19, 24–25, 43
cultural flexibility, 91, 94
culturally relevant pedagogy (CRP), 94, 96

Daily News, 159
decision-makers, 60
deficit-based approaches, for diversity, 28–30
demographics, 30, 51; as antiracism, 79; educational inequality and, 143; gentrification and, 32; racial, 13; shifting, 14; standardized test scores and, 85; "urban schools" and, 7; White students and, 28; zone lines and, 50
Department of Education, 123
Derek (student), 86

desegregation, 1; Civil Rights Act and, 9; court orders, 120; diversity and, 4; material resources and, 5; NAACP and, 8; NYCDOE and, 23; *PICS v. Seattle* and, 27; of public education, 4
Diamond, John, 4, 6, 13, 41, 53, 71–72
Diana, Ms. (assistant principal), 38, 40, 50–51, 55, 57, 60
District 41, 19–22, 25–26, 43–44, 143, 145, 158; Asian American students in, 32; Black students in, 32; Latine students in, 32; NYCDOE and, 15; whiteness and, 31–35; White students in, 32
diversification, 78
diversity: advocacy, 19; antiblackness and, 91; benefits of, 70–73; costs of, 70–73; decision-makers and, 60; deficit-based approaches for, 28–30; defining and not defining, 26–28; desegregation and, 4; exposure to, 132; hidden curriculum of, 4–7, 18; K-301 learning from, 69–70; lessons learned from, 143–46; limits of, 13–14; managing, 40–42; organic diversity, 27, 31; potential, 19, 35–40. *See also specific topics*
"Does the Negro Need Separate Schools?" (Du Bois), 1, 3, 7
Douglass, Frederick, 147
dual-language bilingual classrooms, 33
Du Bois, W. E. B., 2, 5, 96, 105, 119, 139, 144, 146; "Does the Negro Need Separate Schools?," 1, 3, 7; "proper education" and, 32; social equality and, 72
Dumas, Michael, 91, 103

educational inequality, 113, 143
educational justice, 2, 110
educational routines, 82
education policy, assumptions about, 9–13
Egyptian caste system, ancient, 94
ELA. *See* English Language Arts

Elementary and Secondary Education Act, 20
English Language Arts (ELA), 76–77, 95, 100
enrollment policies, 166
equality, social, 72. *See also* inequality
equity: agenda, 141; racial, 98
Evans, Shani, 30
Ewing, Eve L., 11, 12, 29
exposure, to diversity, 132

families of color, 66
Fariña, Carmen, 24–25, 27, 34, 141–42, 165
fears, of community, 158–60
Felix (student), 52, 55, 69
femininity, white, 56
Fine, Michelle, 10
Freire, Paulo, 94, 143
friendships, cross-racial, 90

gender, reputation of students and, 52–54
gentrification, 15, 23, 25, 34, 85
Gibson, Simone, 97
Gifted and Talented program, 22, 149
girls, Black, 53
Gomez, Louis, 53
Gonzalez, Ms. (assistant principal), 40, 44
"good choices," 56
good grades, for Black students, 98–102
goodness, 56, 69
Gordon, Hava Rachel, 25
grade point averages (GPAs), 5
grammar: of M.S. 917, 81–86; neoliberal, 85, 102–4
grassroots advocacy, 142
Greece, Ancient, 87

Hagerman, Margaret, 103, 138
Harlem, New York, 7
Harris, Cheryl, 171n19
Hartmann, Douglas, 25

Hazel (student), 41–42, 52, 69–71, 141, 145, 150, 160, 163; anxiety diagnosis for, 57–59; family of, 60–63; as problem child, 45–49; reputation of, 54–57; self-portrait of, *46*; social norms and, 70
Holloway, Jessica, 97
homework assignments, 122
honor roll students, 98, 99, 101–2
honors classes, 85
hopes, of community, 158–60

identity: adult, 163; racial, 6, 90; student, 87
inequality: educational, 113, 143; racial, 3, 103, 105; social, 84; structural, 6, 127–28, 130; systemic, 114
influential presence, of faculty and administration, 79–80
injustice: awareness of, 129; TTC and, 115
Instagram, 125
Institutional Review Board, 165
integration, 78, 129; advocacy for, 141, 159; diverging lessons in space of, 130–31; hidden curriculum of organizing, 136–39; history of, 79; limits of, 13–14, 104–6; opportunities of, 104–6; transformative, 14; value of, 3. *See also specific topics*
Irby, Decoteau, 79

Janice (parent), 41–42, 44, 48, 68, 71
Jayden (student), 94, 163, 164
justice: educational, 2, 110; racial, 93, 103, 105–6. *See also* injustice

K-301, 51–52, 55, 58, 67, 69–70
Kaden (youth leader), 123
Kaepernick, Colin, 95
Kelvin (youth leader), 123, 125, 134, 135
Kendi, Ibram X., 12
Kimani (parent), 16–17, 19

kindergarteners, 162; enrollment projections, 16; lottery for seats, 22; newcomer families for, 51
King, Martin Luther, Jr., 95, 119
Kirshner, Ben, 123
Klein, Joel, 1, 20, 23
Knox, Ms. (security guard), 49, 62–63, 68
Kucsera, John, 22
Kwon, Soo Ah, 108, 138

Labaree, David, 82
labor, collective, 135
Ladson-Billings, Gloria, 94, 98
Latine students, 1, 5, 16, 62, 89, 131; in District 41, 32; low-income, 2, 20, 28, 33, 39, 43, 49; at M.S. 917, 78; perceptions of, 51; public housing and, 15; "urban schools" demographics and, 7
Lawrence-Lightfoot, Sarah, 163
learned behavior, 64
learning, 14; classroom, 87; K-301, 69–70; peer, 118–22
learning environment, of youth organization, 113–26
Lee, Carol D., 113
"Letter from a Birmingham Jail" (King), 95
Lewis, Amanda, 41, 71–72, 162
"Lift Ev'ry Voice and Sing" ("Black National Anthem"), 91
limit situations, 143
Lina (student), 130
Lipman, Pauline, 21, 97
locus of contestation, 83
low-income students, 2, 20, 28, 30–33, 39, 43, 49, 66, 70
Luna, Nelson, 109

MacLure, Maggie, 52
Maimouna (student), 107–8, 110, 118, 120, 133, 135, 146
Malcolm X, 119

Margot (student), 107–10, 112, 114–15, 123, 125, 131
market-based accountability reforms, 85, 149, 157
Marquise (student), 42, 47–49, 54, 71, 145–46, 160, 163; following instructions, 69; reputation of, 63–68; self-portrait of, 47; social norms and, 70
McGhee, Heather, 148
McGraw, Taylor, 109
McKinney de Royston, Maxine, 104
Medina, Dr. (child psychologist), 57–58, 62, 66
Mehan, Hugh, 10, 162
Mehta, Jal, 82
Mei (student), 129, 139
Melamed, Jodi, 27
Menken, Kate, 33
Merry, Michael, 72, 148
Metz, Mary, 84, 97
Michelle (student), 14, 86–88, 150, 168
middle childhood, 103
middle school orientation, 75–78
model diverse communities, 25
Monika (youth leader), 122, 130, 133, 135, 138
A More Beautiful and Terrible History (Theoharris), 119
M.S. 917, 75–77, 108, 145, 161, 168; as antiracist, integrated school, 78–81; fighting racism, 88–93; grammar of, 81–86; Michelle (student) and, 86–88; race talked about in class, 93–98
multiracial schools, 5
multiracial unity, 92
Myers (Principal), 14, 75–76, 80–81, 94–95, 105–6, 146, 150, 161; on antiracism, 12–13; commitment to antiracism, 78; honor roll and, 101–2; honors classes and, 85; on school norms and rituals, 84; on "teaching for understanding," 83, 96–97; "urban schools" and, 79
"My Family" assignment, 65

NAACP. *See* National Association for the Advancement of Colored People
Nadine (parent), 19
Nancy (parent), 41–42, 44, 46–47, 56, 62–63, 71
Nasir, Na'ilah, 104
Natalie (student), 128–29, 134
National Association for the Advancement of Colored People (NAACP), 8
neighborhood schools, 8, 25, 30
Nelson, Joseph, 53
neoliberal approaches to education, 10, 14, 29
neoliberal grammar, of schooling, 85, 102–4
neoliberalism, 20
neoliberal policy, 20–26
New York City Board of Education, 8
New York City Department of Education (NYCDOE), 17–18, 23, 80, 110, 123–24, 141, 145; choice-based enrollment policies and, 22; District 41 and, 15; dual-language immersion programs and, 33; lottery system of, 22; model diverse communities and, 25; rezoning and, 24; SDAG and, 27; White students and, 8
New York Post, 159
New York Times, 136, 142, 159
No Child Left Behind, 20, 97
Noguera, Pedro, 143
norms, 84; classroom, 63; racialized, 134; social, 70; White, 133–36
NYCDOE. *See* New York City Department of Education
Nygreen, Kysa, 44

official antiracism, 27
Omi, Michael, 6
Orfield, Gary, 21–22, 28
organic diversity, 27, 31
Orozco, Ms. (special education coordinator), 64

O'Shea, Ms. (teacher), 39, 51, 70, 161; Hazel and, 46, 52, 54–58, 60–62; Marquise and, 48, 63–65, 67–69

parent activism, 8
parenting practices, of women of color, 62
Paris, Django, 101
Pascoe, C. J., 84
Paula (student), 129, 130
peer teaching and learning, 118–22
pen pals, 26
perceptions, of Black and Latine students, 51
"per pupil" funds, 35
Phillippo, Kate, 10, 137
PICS v. Seattle, 27–28
"places of refuge," 108
policy actors: policy targets and, 122–26; teachers as, 10
policy targets, 122–26
political advocacy, 109–10
politics of care, 84
Posey-Maddox, Linn, 25, 30, 43
positive role models, 56
potential diversity, 19, 35–40
poverty, 148. *See also* low-income students
powell, john a., 14
power, social, 87; Teens Take Charge and, 118, 123, 126, 136, 138
priority groups, for admissions, 28
problem children (children with problems), 45–48; costs and benefits of diversity for, 70–73; Hazel's anxiety diagnosis, 57–59; Hazel's family, 60–63; Hazel's reputation, 54–57; Marquise's reputation, 63–68; reputation of, 52–54; staff and children at P.S. 411, 49–52
"proper education," 32, 43, 79
protests, 8
P.S. 411, 16–17, 25, 29, 47, 145, 150, 161, 168; as default destination, 15; demographic changes and, 18; diversity management and, 40–42; potential diversity at, 35–40; rezoning of, 35–37, 39–40, 158; staff and students of, 49–52; whiteness and, 43–44; zone lines, 50
"P.S. 411 and Me" workshops, 37
public education: desegregation of, 4; M.S. 917 as alternative to, 85; pushing limits of, 106, 146; racism in, 81
public housing, 60, 66
public policy, 139
public school system, 8, 13, 108, 143, 149

race, 73; critical race theory, 9; reputation of students and, 52–54; talked about in class, 93–98
Race in the Schoolyard (Lewis), 162
racial bias, 12, 72
racial demographics, 13
racial equity, 98
racial identity, 6, 90
racial inequality, 3, 103, 105
racialized norms, 100, 134
racialized organizations, 83
racial justice, 93, 103, 105–6
racial projects, 6, 162
racial tensions, 116
racism, 11, 37, 138, 148; fighting, 88–93, 145, 146; in public education, 81; systemic, 10. *See also* antiracism
radical care, 83
Radical Possibilities (Anyon), 144
Ramona (student), 131, 132
Ray, Victor, 83
real estate, 171n19
redistributing, of resources, 6
reforms. *See* accountability reforms
Regina (student), 134
reputation of students: gender and, 52–54; of Hazel, 54–57; of Marquise, 63–68; race and, 52–54

rezoning, 29–30; gentrification and, 42; meeting for, 16, 25, 44; NYCDOE proposing, 24; of P.S. 411, 35–37, 39–40, 158
Ridgeway, Cecilia, 53
Rivera-McCutcheon, Rosa, 83
Roberts, John (Chief Justice), 27
role models, positive, 56
Rosen, Sonia, 137
ross, kihana, 83
Royal, Camika, 97

San Francisco Bay Area, 157
school choice, 21–23
School Colors (podcast), 159
School Diversity Advisory Group (SDAG), 27
school marketplace, 20–26
school strike, 124, *124*
SDAG. *See* School Diversity Advisory Group
segregation, 89, 108; starting points of, 126–30; youth organization against, 109–13. *See also specific topics*
Seif, Mr. (teacher), 76, 100
self-portrait assignment, 45, *46*
Shalaby, Carla, 70, 150
Shange, Savannah, 101
Shonda (staff member), 34–35
Sienna (student), 127
sister schools program, 26
skills: academic, 121; advocacy, 139; civil, 113–14
slavery, 93
Smith, Ms. (teacher), 39
social change, 122
social equality, 72
social inequality, 84
social location, 159
social media, 38
social norms, 70
social power, 87

social studies, 137
Sojoyner, Damian, 82
Spanish Civil War, 92
special education, 66
standardized test scores, 85, 94
status quo, 8, 84, 146
Stephenson, Whitney, 109
Stockstill, Casey, 148
structural inequality, 6, 127–28, 130
student identity, 87
Stulberg, Lisa, 157
Supreme Court: *Brown v. Board of Education*, 4, 6, 8, 11, 26, 43, 83, 112; *PICS v. Seattle*, 27–28
systemic inequality, 114
systemic racism, 10

"talking piece," 77
Tanner, Ms. (teacher), 40
Tatum, Beverly Daniel, 90
teachers: blamed for social problems, 12; as policy actors, 10; of P.S. 411, 49–52. *See also specific teachers*
Teach for America, 134
teaching, 14; peer, 118–22; for understanding, 83, 96–97
Teens Take Charge (TTC), 107, 108, 129–36, 142, 146, 150–51, 164–68; Amina and, 117–18; Asian American students in, 175n6 (chap. 4); "check-in" at, 114; cultural flexibility of, 139; exposure to racial diversity, 132; injustice and, 115; peer teaching and learning in, 118–22; policy change and, 113; policy targets and policy actors, 122–26; press conference, *121*; as proof of concept, 131; rally, *111*; reasons for joining, 118; against school segregation, 109–13; school strike, *124*; strategy sessions of, 165; structural inequality and, 127–28, 130
Teen Vogue, 136

Tello, Mr. (student), 87–88, 90, 92–93, 96–97
temper tantrums, 59
Theoharris, Jeanne, 119
Tobin, William, 81
transformative integration, 14
Trump, Donald, 94–95
TTC. *See* Teens Take Charge
Turner, Erica, 25, 35, 43
Twitter, 125
Tyack, David, 81

UCLA Civil Rights Project, 9, 21–22, 31
Underground Railroad, 92, 96, 97
underperforming, schools as, 20
urban amenities, diverse schools as, 23–26
urban development, 24
"urban schools," 7–8

"Wealthy White Manhattan Parents Angrily Rant against Plan to Bring More Black Kids to Their Schools" (video), 1
Weis, Lois, 10
Wells, Amy Stuart, 29
WhatsApp, 122, 166
White backlash, 30
White families, 13
white femininity, 56
white flight, 9
whiteness, 15–19, 146; dilemma of, 43–44; District 41 rebranded, 31–35; diversity management and, 40–42; neoliberal policy and, 20–26; potential diversity at PS. 411, 35–40; school diversity defined, 26–30; school marketplace and, 20–26
White norms, 133–36
White students, 5, 35, 50, 89, 127, 132; *Brown v. Board of Education* and, 4; in District 41, 32; gentrification and, 22; at M.S. 917, 79; NYCDOE and, 8; "urban schools" demographics and, 8
white supremacy, 4, 6, 82, 94, 146, 148
White Teens Take Charge, 138
Why Are All the Black Kids Sitting Together in the Cafeteria? (Tatum), 90
Williams, Mr. (parent coordinator), 49–50, 63, 67
Winant, Howard, 6
women of color, parenting practices of, 62
Wortham, Stanton, 87

X, Malcolm, 119

youth organization, 107–8, 164–67; learning environment of, 113–26; against school segregation, 109–13. *See also* Teens Take Charge

Zaloom, Caitlin, 157
Zoë (student), 130
zone lines, 24; Amina on, 117; changes to, 15–16, 50; P.S. 411, 50. *See also* rezoning
Zoom, 116, 117, 142, 165, 166

ABOUT THE AUTHOR

ALEXANDRA FREIDUS is Assistant Professor of Educational Leadership at the University of Connecticut. Her ethnographic research examines how students, educators, families, and policy makers conceptualize racial inequality, enact educational policy, and influence teaching and learning.